Erica Wilson's
NEEDLEWORK
TO WEAR

Erica Wilson's
NEEDLEWORK TO WEAR

OXMOOR HOUSE, INC. BIRMINGHAM

Library of Congress Catalog Number: 82-80595
ISBN: 0-8487-0527-0
Manufactured in the United States of America
First Printing 1982

ISBN 0-8487-0527-0

CONTENTS

INTRODUCTION

Exquisite needlework has always been a most important part of fashion. In fact, historically, handmade things were more than just a *part*—they were all of it. Mass-produced clothing of the twentieth century may have put us into plain work clothes, but now needlework is flowering once again and beautiful, one-of-a-kind clothes and accessories are appearing everywhere. Their classic designs will surely be enjoyed by future generations just as much as we appreciate our grandmothers' clothes today.

Because the real expense is the time and skill of your own hands, you can afford to find extravagantly beautiful materials. You can combine your handmade jewelry with semi-precious stones such as lapiz lazuli, carnelian and garnets, and for your clothing you can use fabrics such as silk, suede, and cashmere. Or, besides enriching your wardrobe with these sublime creations, you can find a simple, inexpensive garment and, with a few swift techniques, give it a luxurious elegance. Even if you use everyday fabrics, your stitches can transform the garment into a work of art. If you are embarking on a time-consuming heirloom, though, it is worth your while to use the best materials; they will cost a fraction of what ready-made items would in the same materials.

In the following pages, I will show you how to make gold jewelry, heirloom lacy blouses, jeweled belts, beaded collars, and cross-stitch handbags with the look of lace. You can make medallions inspired by Celtic ornaments or hammered gold bands like those from the ancient cultures of almost every country. Make a chaplet of golden leaves like one made in the royal Sumerian workshops thousands of years before Christ. Or learn smocking—it's not just for *little* girls. Make a painted, quilted silk jacket, a magnificent Victorian evening skirt, a woven ribbon handbag.

This book is designed to show you how easy it can be, with the right materials at your disposal, to discover a whole new world. At the end of the book, you'll find a list of suppliers for any materials you have trouble finding. Also there are diagrams of stitches you may not know and other information on techniques that will help you make maximum use of this volume.

You can easily enrich your wardrobe with your own creative touches, acquiring ideas for quick and easy ways to decorate an existing garment or to make clothing and accessories. These things can truly become heirlooms because fashion trends may change as quickly as the wind, but handmade things of good craftsmanship have a classic quality that goes on forever.

Portrait of Mary Cornwallis by George Gower. (City Art Gallery, Manchester, England.)

JEWELRY

Sixteenth century portrait of Queen Elizabeth I by Nicholas Hillyarde.

From the Treasures of Tutankhamen to the graceful forms of art nouveau, from the ancient Sumerian workshops to the graphic simplicity of contemporary masterpieces, the whole sweep of design for jewelry can be yours to interpret with your needle. The ideas on the next pages are like the tip of the iceberg. As you master the techniques, you will find new ideas, some intricate, and some amazingly simple.

The organdy dogwood blossoms opposite were inspired by an Italian necklace made in rock crystal and gold with blue diamond centers. They are photographed close up on a field of gold couching. This technique of covering the entire fabric with swirls of real gold thread originated in China, where the art of needlework has always been considered equal to painting and sculpture.

One of the most extraordinary things about gold is that the techniques of craftsmanship are the same today as they were thousands of years ago. The ring you wear may have been formed in the lost wax method known for at least four thousand years, and today you can do your embroidery with a gold thread produced in the same method as that used by the Chinese since time immemorial.

The gold was wrapped around silver bullion, which was melted down and drawn through narrower and narrower holes until, still coated with gold, it formed a thin wire. This flexible thread was then beaten flat and twisted around a core of orange or yellow silk. Nowadays, gold leaf on paper is twisted around and lightly gummed to the silk, and the thread is known as Japanese gold. Flexible, untarnishing, and of a beautiful glowing color, Japanese gold can only be couched on the surface of fabric, as it would naturally be spoiled by pulling it back and forth through cloth.

This real gold thread is still obtainable, both in gold and in silver gilt. But the same production methods are applied to aluminum and lurex, so you can choose your thread according to your purse and the final use of your needlework.

As well as gold, you can work with ribbons, silk floss, and fabric. You can work on suede cloth, on needlepoint canvas and on organdy, and you will become intrigued with the almost limitless possibilities.

You will see the Ecuador gold necklace on page 32, for instance, used as the clasp for a handbag on page 84. In the same way, the Viking medallion on page 28 would look marvelous repeated five or six times and strung on leather thongs to make a belt, and the leaves on page 34 could be made in miniature to be used as earrings. You can combine your gold embroidery with precious stones or silken cords you have made yourself. Although you will find specific instructions for all kinds of jewelry in this chapter, use your own ideas to combine things in different ways, giving each one that special touch that will make it your own.

Chain stitch in fine gold thread outline the organdy petals of these DOGWOOD BLOSSOMS. Centers are encircled with miniature rhinestones.

Above: Swirls of gold are couched on fabric to make a HAMMERED GOLD BAND of Celtic design.

Above left: CHAPLET OF LEAVES inspired by one made in Ancient Mesopotamia.

Above: GOLD RIBBON RUFF. From left: EGYPTIAN CRESCENT and ECUADOR GOLD MEDALLION in needlepoint highlighted with gold threads. Couched gold cord makes a VIKING MEDALLION.

These RIBBON BRACELETS can be made in any color with the simple technique of lanyard weaving.

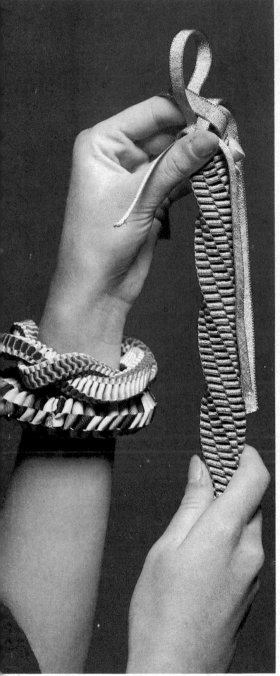

Below: MACRAME NECKLACE with carrick bend medallion. Opposite: CLIMBING ROPE BRACELETS in a whole array of colors.

Left and lower left: Embroidered BUTTERFLY NECKLACE.
Below and center opposite: Puffy POLKA-DOT PANSIES.

12

Upper right: ROSE MEDALLION. Lower
right: BUTTERFLY MEDALLION. Lower left:
CROSS-STITCH HEART.

FLOWERING BRANCH NECKLACE

This delicate apple blossom necklace was made by Mira Green in a unique three-dimensional technique she has perfected. Although the original necklace was made on forty-mesh gauze, individual flowers can be counted from the graphs and used on canvas of a larger scale for a corsage, lapel pin, or hair ornament. If you use the graphs, any canvas larger than thirty-mesh will make the flowers too large for a necklace; if you wish to use a coarser mesh, trace the full-size petals and leaves from this page instead. Remember, though, that mono canvas is not suitable, as it is too thick and inflexible. The ideal materials are silk or nylon gauze or Penelope canvas.

The variations in design for this technique are almost limitless. Flower heads such as pansies, daises, morning glories, or dogwood blossoms could be your inspiration, or you could use shells, butterflies, or leaves as your theme. The necklace would also be attractive made entirely from fabric.

With a Trace Erase™ pen, mark out the area for each petal and leaf on the gauze, using the graphs as your guide. Follow the photo, making five petals for each flower and three for each bud, or make your own arrangement. Leave at least

SHOPPING LIST
40-count gauze, silk or nylon mesh
  up to 30-count or
  Penelope canvas (2/24 or 4/28)
floss or yarn for leaves and petals
all-purpose glue
strong, thin florist's wire
iron-on fabric in white or a color to
  match needlepoint
acrylic paints
permanent sharp-point marking pens
  in colors to match needlepoint
stamens for silk flowers
aluminum foil
polymer resin

LEAVES

FULL-SIZE PATTERNS

PETAL

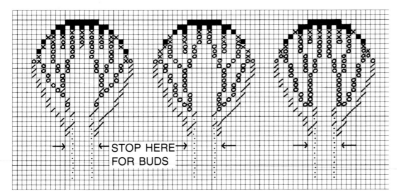

←STOP HERE→
FOR BUDS

PETAL GRAPHS

■ DARKEST
✗
⊠
◪
⬚ LIGHTEST

LEAF
GRAPHS

eight threads between each shape to allow for turnbacks. Work in tent stitch, using one strand of floss for 40-mesh gauze (or more, according to your mesh size). Note that the lower portion of each shape is left free of stitching.

Cut out the completed pieces, allowing approximately four threads around each for turnbacks. Place each leaf or petal face down and apply a small amount of glue around all edges except the unworked section at the base, using a toothpick. Allow the glue to dry; apply a second coat and turn back the glued edges smoothly to the reverse side.

Measure wire to fit behind the center of each petal and extend for a stem. Now you are ready to use your iron-on fabric; if a coordinating color is not available, tone white fabric with acrylic paints to blend with the needlepoint.

Put a square of aluminum foil on the ironing board and place a completed petal face down on it. Place the length of wire on the back of the petal so that it lies in the center with the long stem of wire projecting at the base. Place a square of iron-on backing, shiny side down, on top of the petal so that it extends on all sides except the base.

Fuse the three layers together with a hot iron. Trim away the excess backing flush to the needlepoint petal. Re-fuse edges if necessary and touch up any bare spots left on the canvas with a sharp-pointed marker in an appropriate shade. You will have a petal in needlepoint with fabric backing and a wire stem, ready for wrapping and joining with other petals to make a flower.

Place a dab of glue on the canvas at the base of each shape. Allow it to dry, apply a second coat, and fold unworked canvas around the wire. After drying, wrap the unworked area with floss, continuing down the stem until the desired length is reached. Repeat this procedure for all petals and leaves.

To make flowers, assemble any combination of five petals with a few stamens in the center, needlepoint sides facing *in*. Wrap all stem wires together with floss and bend petals outward to shape the flower.

To make buds, combine shortened versions of all three petals, needlepoint facing *out,* with a few stamens in the center. Wrap the stems as you did the flowers, but bend the petals inward.

Assemble a pleasing combination of buds, flowers, and leaves and wrap their stems to one another with floss to create a branched effect. Attach the flowering branch to a neck band by wrapping.

To make a realistic dew drop, build up drops of clear polymer resin on aluminum foil and, when dry, glue them in place. (Do not drop the resin directly onto the needlepoint or it will be absorbed.)

BUTTERFLY NECKLACE

This technique for making freestanding butterflies with organdy can be effective in many shapes, such as shells, flowers, leaves, etc. You can use a single shape as a pin or appliqué several to a sweater, collar, or dress.

To trace the full-size patterns from this page, mount organdy in an embroidery frame and outline the designs, tracing them through the organdy with a hard pencil or with a Trace Erase™ pen. Embroider by following the charts here, using two strands of cotton floss; consult the photograph on page 13 for your color scheme. Fill all wings with close stitching such as Roumanian, Oriental Laid Work (Diagram 1), and satin stitch first. Then outline each section with split stitch and add satin stitch on top afterwards. Finally, work buttonhole stitch around the edges, loops to the outside. Alternatively, the butterflies could be made in needlepoint, similar to the flowering branch necklace on the previous page.

To stiffen the organdy, moisten the reverse side of the wings with all-purpose glue, especially around the edges. When dry, carefully cut the organdy around the wings flush against the buttonhole edge. Closely wrap a doubled (2½"-long) pipe cleaner or piece of candlewicking with black cotton floss and bend it back over the center of the wings to form the body. For antennae, strip paper from twist-ties and closely wrap them with cotton floss. Knot the ends to form a strip 3" long and fold it in half, attaching it to the head by slipping it under the upper end of the body.

For a neckband, twist together enough pipe cleaners to measure 17" or cut a 17"-long piece of candlewicking. Form a loop on one end and a hook on the other. Wrap closely with six strands of cotton floss. Attach the butterflies securely, positioning them as in the photograph.

(Color photo, page 13.)

SHOPPING LIST
¼ yard organdy
embroidery frame
hard pencil or Trace Erase™ pen
cotton floss
all-purpose glue
pipe cleaners or metal-core
  candlewicking
plastic bag twist-ties

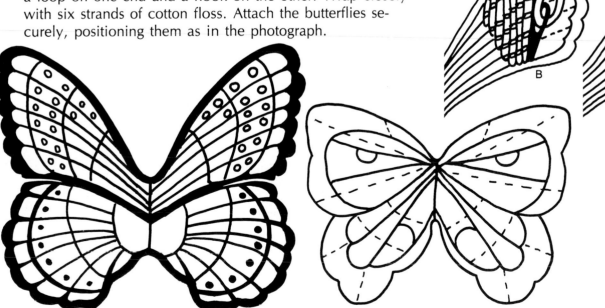

(Color photo, page 13.)

POLKA-DOT PANSIES

SHOPPING LIST
scraps of 100% cotton or cotton
    batiste fabric in gingham,
    calico, polka dots, and prints
cotton floss
loose cotton batting or lamb's wool
choker

Heartsease is the charming English name for wild minia-ture pansies, and these dancing polka-dot flowers seem to represent the name perfectly. Five of them on a clasped ring make a circle necklace; smaller versions could be used indi-vidually for earrings.

Trace the full-size patterns here onto doubled fabric, right sides facing (Diagram 1). Stitch the two pieces for the pansy front together, right sides facing, using the smallest stitch available on the machine or using tiny backstitches by hand. Leave a small opening between the stars marked on the pat-tern for turning the piece right side out. Trim ¼" away from the stitches. Clip and notch turnbacks, turn right side out, stuff with batting or lamb's wool (Diagram 2) and slip stitch closed. Make the pansy back in the same way.

For the puffy pansy effect, pinch and whip stitch the re-verse side of each flower front, oversewing tightly to "dim-ple" the petals (Diagram 3). Repeat for the back of the pansy, but push stuffing to the tops of the petals, pinch, and stitch tightly at the dotted lines shown on full-size patterns (Diagram 4).

Work leaves in the same method, again holding stuffing at the top of the leaf, stitching the base along the dotted lines, and pinching to form a folded vein in the leaf.

Now add embroidery touches to the front of the pansy. With two strands of cotton floss, work three sets of three

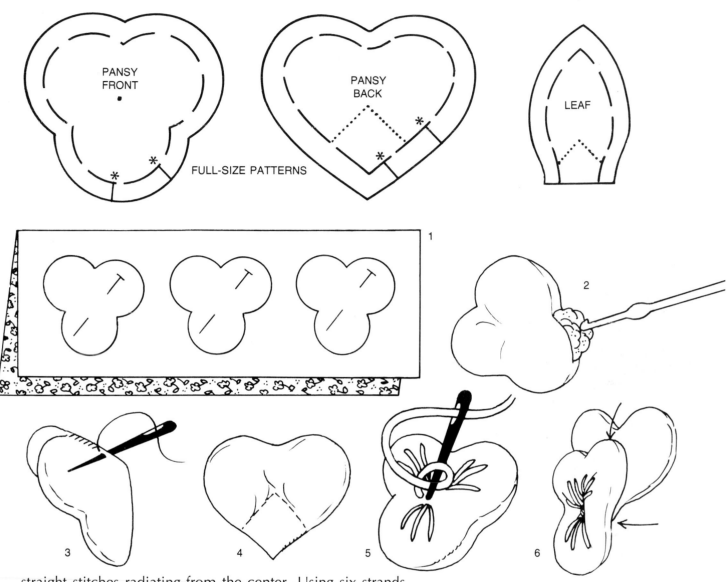

FULL-SIZE PATTERNS

straight stitches radiating from the center. Using six strands, work one French knot in the center (Diagram 5).

With tiny stitches, securely join the back to the front at arrows (Diagram 6). This leaves a space between petals through which to slip the neckband. Join the leaves to the flowers (Diagram 7) and thread a store-bought choker band or a ribbon through the center of each flower.

Some important tricks for good results in making both the pansies and the heart on the next page:

Open and flatten seams before turning them right side out.

Leave the opening for turning on one side, never at an awkward point at the top or bottom.

Stuff well into corners. Lamb's wool is best because it is springier and more resilient than loose batting.

Fold over and stitch pleats at the back for a puffy, rounded effect in front.

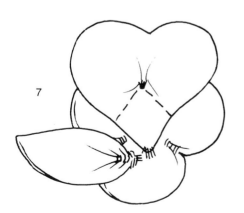

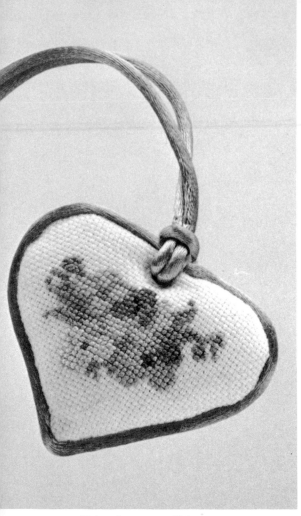

(Color photo, page 13.)

CROSS-STITCH HEART

Tiny heartsease pansies are cross-stitched on Aida cloth to make a pendant. Whatever color scheme you choose, pick up the predominating color for the cord outlining the heart. Instead of lamb's wool, you may prefer to stuff the heart with potpourri to make a sweet-smelling nosegay.

Trace two full-size patterns from page 21 onto fabric. Counting from the center point marked on the graph, cross-stitch the floral design inside the heart outline, using two strands of cotton floss and #20 tapestry needle.

Cut out the heart shapes and sew them together, right sides facing, leaving an opening for stuffing. Trim seams, cutting notches around curves, and open up seams, pressing them flat with your finger and thumb to give a clean edge (Diagram 1).

Turn the heart right side out, stuff with lamb's wool, and insert upholstery weights (Diagram 2). Be sure to stuff well into the curved shoulders of the heart and down into the point. Blind stitch the opening and outline the heart with the rattail cord, carefully hemming with invisible stitches.

Carefully poke an opening through the top of the heart with the closed points of scissors. Loop the remaining rattail cord through the hole and draw tight to form hanger (Diagram 3).

SHOPPING LIST
1 (8″ × 10″) piece of 22-count Aida cloth
cotton floss
lamb's wool
upholstery weights
2 yards of rattail cord

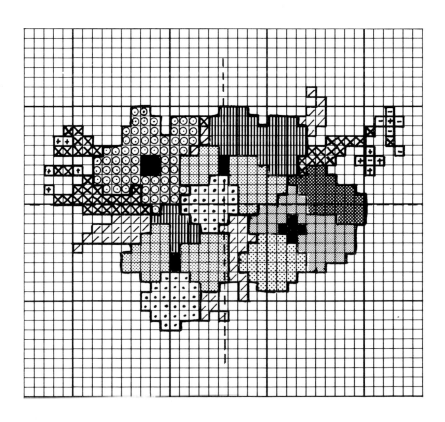

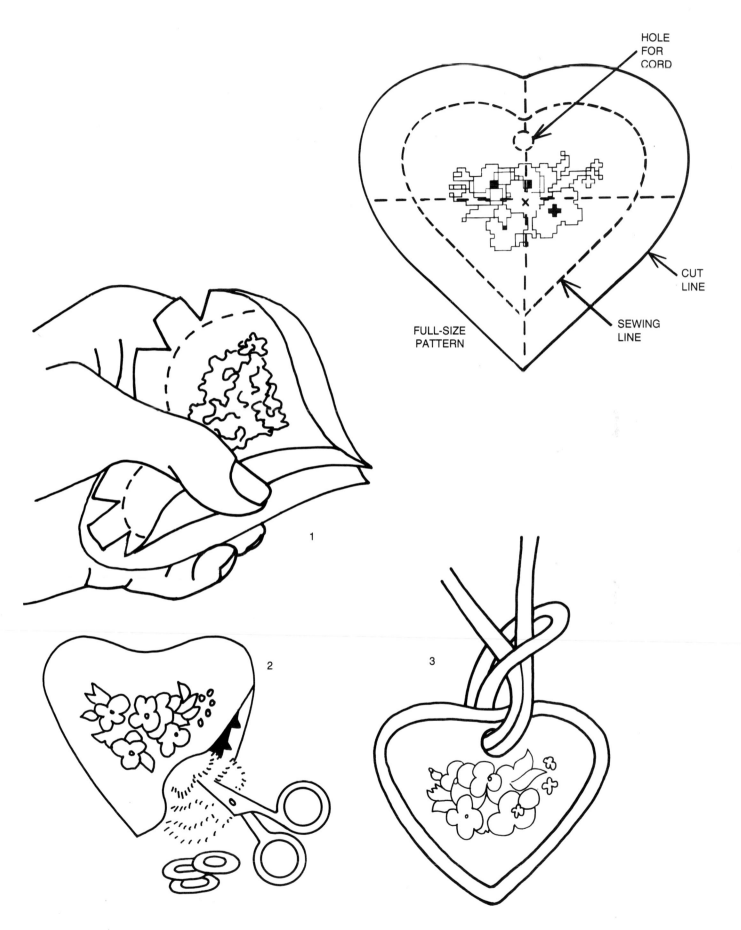

HOLE
FOR
CORD

CUT
LINE

SEWING
LINE

FULL-SIZE
PATTERN

1

2

3

MACRAME NECKLACE

This necklace is made in one continuous piece, working the neckband first and then knotting the loose ends for the central medallion.

Place nails or tee pins approximately ½" apart. Cut six (6 yard) lengths of cord, three in each color. Knot one strand of cord to each nail, leaving approximately 18" of loose cord on top, which will later form the central medallion. Use the following color sequence, from left to right: one dark strand, one light, two dark, one light, and one dark.

Begin with the square knot, which is done in two steps. Using the four center cords only, bring the right cord (E) over to the left of the two center cords (C and D) and under the left cord (B). Then bring the left cord (B) under the center cords (C and D) and through the loop at the right cord (E). Pull to form the first half of the knot. (Diagram 1.)

To form the second half of the knot, take the left cord (E) over and to the right of the center cords, under the right cord (B). Then bring the right cord under the center cords and through the loop of the left cord (Diagram 2). Pull for the finished knot (Diagram 3).

The next row is worked in two square knots, using the three left cords (A, B, and C) for the first knot and the three right cords (D, E and F) for the second knot. Note that because you are using only three cords, there is only one center cord. (Diagram 4.)

Repeat this pattern (one row with a centered square knot, one row of two square knots) until you have a total of eleven rows. The last row will be a centered knot.

Using all six cords, work a carrick bend. Make a loop as shown, using the three left cords (Diagram 5). Now wind through the three right cords in a figure eight motion, following the arrows in Diagram 6.

Repeat from the beginning (eleven rows of square knots, one carrick bend) three times. End with eleven rows of square knots, omitting the last carrick bend.

Remove the knots from the nails and use all twelve strands from both ends to finish the necklace with one large carrick bend at the base. Trim loose strands to approximately three inches each and wrap their ends with a contrasting shade of floss. Lightly glue the overlapping cords flat on the central carrick bend to prevent them from twisting.

SHOPPING LIST
2 contrasting colors (18 yards each) of macrame cord
macrame board and tee pins or board and nails
cotton floss

(Color photo, page 10.)

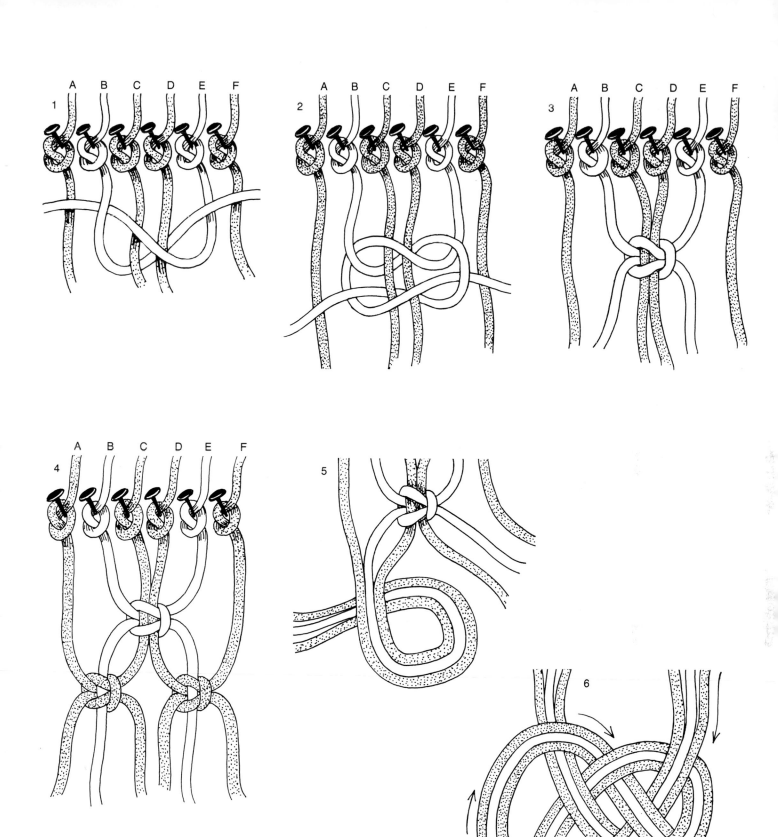

(Color photo, page 11.)

SHOPPING LIST
9" to 10" (⅜"-thick) tensile
  climbing rope in any color
⅛"-thick climbing rope for joining
cotton floss
all-purpose glue

CLIMBING ROPE BRACELETS

Climbing rope for these colorful bracelets designed and made by Jessica Cushman can be found at your local sporting goods store. All you have to do is cut the rope, sew its ends together, and glue thinner rope in a contrasting color over the join.

Begin by wrapping floss around the rope on both sides of the section to be cut to prevent fraying. (The length for an average wrist is 9"-10".) Stitch the two wrapped ends together, joining the woven rayon outer skin (Diagram 1). Alternatively, you may prefer to cut and fuse the rope with a soldering iron or hot knife. To conceal the join, glue and stitch three wrappings of the thinner rope over it (Diagram 2).

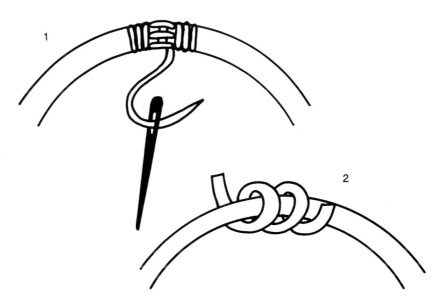

RIBBON BRACELETS

SHOPPING LIST
4 pieces (each approximately
  2 yards long) ¼"-wide novelty
  double-faced ribbon

These ribbon bracelets can be made in spectacular colors to match any outfit. They are quickly and easily done on the principle of lanyard weaving. Those shown here, designed and made by Ruth Katz, would be equally attractive used as belts or necklaces.

Double-faced ribbon is necessary, since both sides show in the finished piece. The thinner the width of the ribbon, the less yardage you will need.

To give yourself the shortest possible working pieces of ribbon, find the centers of the four pieces that are to be worked. Lay them out, layering them over each other as shown. Lightly tack them together to hold them in position. (Diagram 1.)

Working in a counterclockwise direction, fold the ribbons over one another. Begin with A over D (Diagram 2). Then fold B over A; C over B; and, finally, D over C and under the loop formed by A (Diagram 3). Tighten the ends after each round.

Now, following on Diagram 3, work in a clockwise direction and fold D over A; C over D; and B over C; and, finally, thread A over B and through the loop formed by D. This returns the ribbons to their original positions.

(Color photo, page 8.)

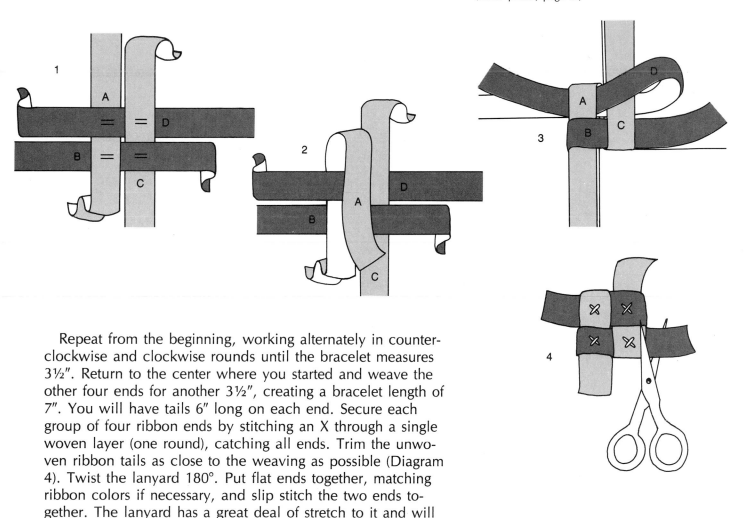

Repeat from the beginning, working alternately in counterclockwise and clockwise rounds until the bracelet measures 3½". Return to the center where you started and weave the other four ends for another 3½", creating a bracelet length of 7". You will have tails 6" long on each end. Secure each group of four ribbon ends by stitching an X through a single woven layer (one round), catching all ends. Trim the unwoven ribbon tails as close to the weaving as possible (Diagram 4). Twist the lanyard 180°. Put flat ends together, matching ribbon colors if necessary, and slip stitch the two ends together. The lanyard has a great deal of stretch to it and will return to its shape even after you've stretched it to get it over your wrist.

(Color photo, page 6.)

EGYPTIAN CRESCENT

From Tutankhamen's tomb came craftsmanship that astounded the world. The shape of this needlepoint is typical of Egyptian ornament, and is combined with garnet and gold beads. With this idea, you could make eagles, lotus blossoms, scarabs, or, closer at hand, sea horses, fish, or horses' heads in needlepoint, outlining the shapes in gold buttonhole stitch.

To prepare your canvas for accurate placement of the design, fold it in half vertically, right down the center, and repeat this horizontally. Mark these crease lines by running a pencil lightly between the threads of the canvas, allowing the threads to guide you in keeping the lines straight. Pull the pencil across the canvas rather than push it; you will find it will easily stay between the threads without running off the line. With a waterproof marker, trace the full-size pattern onto the canvas, aligning the vertical and horizontal lines with the threads of the canvas.

Following the color scheme in the photograph on page 6, or using your own color selection, work the entire inner semicircle with the lighter color of floss and the outer semicircle with the darker color, both in tent stitch. On #16 canvas, use four strands of cotton floss. (Diagram 1.)

With two threads of Fil d'Or and a large chenille needle (to protect the gold as it passes through the canvas), work herringbone stitch around both semicircles. You'll be working right over the needlepoint, leaving a gap between the two rows. (Diagram 2.)

Thread beads on nylon cord and attach them to the upper edge of the canvas. Adjust them so that six rows of beads lie evenly, side by side.

Now outline the medallion as shown (Diagram 3). Starting with a line between the two semicircles, buttonhole neatly over heavy gold cord with two threads of Fil d'Or. Then, starting at one inside corner, buttonhole over cord along one upper edge, around the outside edge, and along the opposite upper edge.

Trace the pattern onto plastic and cut out. Trim canvas, leaving ¼" turnbacks. Notch and fold edges over plastic and glue (Diagram 4). Buttonhole over the curtain ring and attach it with tiny stitches.

Tape the upholstery weight in position at the center of the reverse side.

Trace and cut the pattern piece from fusible interfacing. Fuse interfacing to backing fabric with a hot iron. Trim, clipping and notching turnbacks. Slip stitch backing to the completed medallion.

SHOPPING LIST
square of #16 canvas
cotton floss in two shades
DMC Fil d'Or (fine Lurex thread)
gold beads
garnet beads
nylon cord
heavy gold cord
lightweight plastic (as used for file folders)
all-purpose glue
1 (1⅜"-diameter) curtain ring
upholstery weight
fusible interfacing
cotton or silk fabric for backing

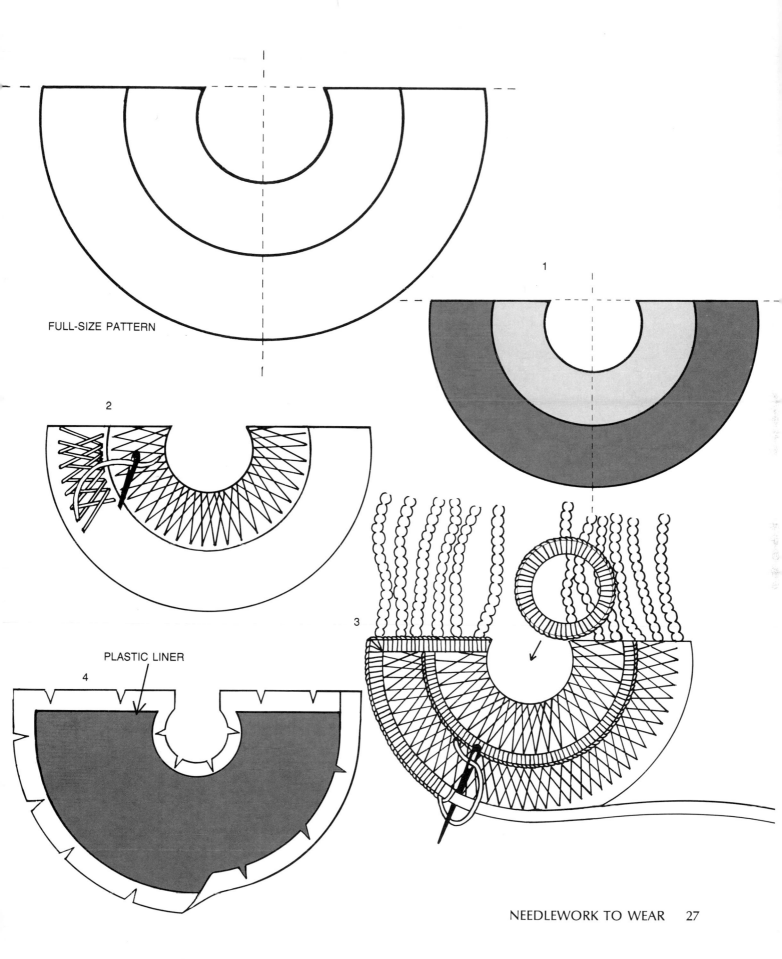

FULL-SIZE PATTERN

1

2

3

PLASTIC LINER

4

VIKING MEDALLION

(Color photo, page 7.)

SHOPPING LIST
¼ yard suede cloth
metallic gold cord
Maltese sewing silk ("horsetail")
beeswax
sequins
gold beads (optional)
gold silk cord
lightweight plastic (as used for
  file folders)
upholstery weight
all-purpose glue

Viking filigree work was done with fine gold or silver wires, sometimes ornamented to resemble strings of beads. These were twisted and then soldered to a surface, often bronze, to provide contrast with the gold or silver. Rings, brooches, and cloak pins of this design were worn equally by Viking men and women.

Since the original work was done by twisting threads, the design is a natural for needlework. Ideal for a pendant, several of these medallions could be strung on leather thongs to make a western-style belt.

Transfer full-size patterns onto suede cloth. Dots on the pattern indicate the points of the diamond.

Mount the fabric on stretcher strips or in an embroidery hoop. Lay metallic cord in the basic diamond shape, securing it with silk thread only at the four corners denoted by the dots on the pattern. Plunge ends through to the back at the upper point of the diamond with a large chenille or tapestry needle.

Using a blunt tapestry needle or your fingers, loop metallic cord under and over the diamond (Diagram 1). Couch down loops with waxed silk thread and plunge the ends of the cord under one of the arms of the diamond to make an invisible join.

Sew down sequins, holding them in place with one gold bead or french knot in the center. Couch two rows of metallic cord and one row of silk cord around the perimeter of the circle, plunging ends at different points.

To make the loop to hold the medallion as illustrated, couch one row of silk cord lengthwise on the center of the rectangle, with two rows of metallic cord on either side of it.

To mount, encircle the medallion with two rows of gathering threads just outside the original outline. Cut a plastic liner from the full-size pattern, tape an upholstery weight to it, and insert it in the fabric circle. Draw up the gathering threads. Repeat this procedure for the backing.

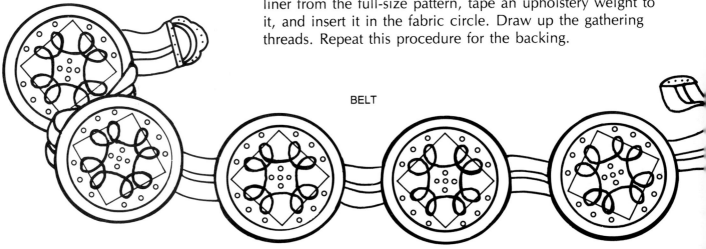

BELT

FULL-SIZE PATTERN FOR MEDALLION

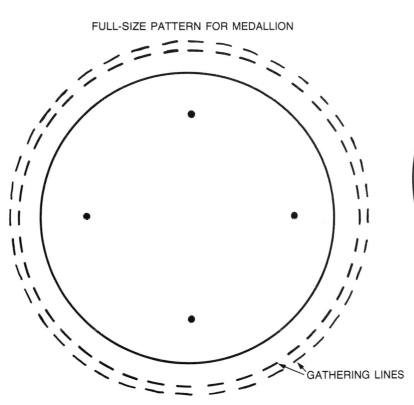

GATHERING LINES

1

Cut out the rectangle for the loop or hanger, leaving ¼" turnbacks all around. Glue down turnbacks on either side. Fold over the rectangle and glue its ends together, making sure that two thicknesses of silk cord can pass through the tube thus formed. Glue the hanger in position on the reverse side above one of the points of the diamond. Glue the backing over it.

Measure the desired length of silk cord for the necklace. Double it and pass it through the hanger. Stitch a loop at one end of the cord. Coil, knot, and stitch the other end so that the coil, when passed through the loop, will secure the necklace.

FULL-SIZE PATTERN FOR LOOP

TURN BACK   THICK CORD   TURN BACK

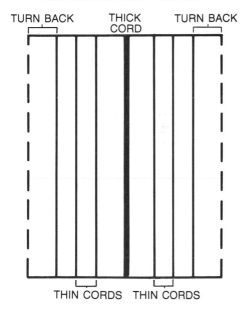

THIN CORDS   THIN CORDS

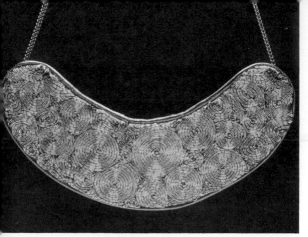

(Color photo, page 5.)

SHOPPING LIST
natural linen fabric
Maltese sewing silk ("horsetail")
beeswax
Japanese gold thread
lightweight plastic (as used for
  file folders)
crinoline (optional)
all-purpose glue
gold knit jersey fabric (optional)
suede cloth
#10 crewel needles
#18 tapestry needle

HAMMERED GOLD BAND

This golden band is shaped like the hammered gold neck ornaments found in most ancient cultures. The simple design shows the beauty of the real gold thread, changing color as it swirls around. Follow exactly the pattern shown here, or cut out your own from thin cardboard and try it on for size before you begin. The gold couching will easily fill any shape from crescent to bow, so, since you are making it yourself, you can fit it perfectly to your neckline.

A good way to balance your design is to first sketch the outline on graph paper, counting the squares to be sure that both sides are alike. Glue the graph paper to plastic and cut both out together. Lay the plastic pattern on the linen, trace around it with a permanent marker or Trace Erase™, mount the fabric in an embroidery frame, and you are ready to begin couching.

Measure a strand of Japanese gold that is twice as long as necessary to complete two circles. Fold it in half and, with waxed silk thread, sew the looped end onto the dot marking the center of a circle. Couch round and round (Diagram 1). For placement of your couching stitches, either follow radiating lines you have marked on the fabric or "brick" the stitches, placing the stitches in each succeeding row halfway between those in the previous row. You can also work as shown in the photograph, radiating the stitches from the center of each circle in a random manner, without marked lines to guide you.

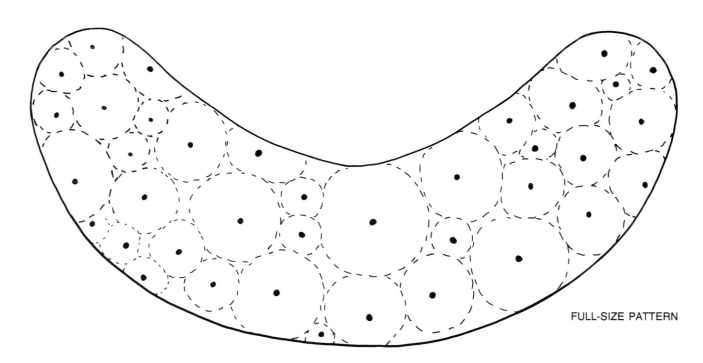

FULL-SIZE PATTERN

Begin in the center of a circle, working round and round from the center so that the double rows of gold lie flat, side by side. When you reach the outside of the circle, continue on to the outside of the next, this time working your way in, round and round towards the center (Diagram 2). Always bring the needle up on the outside of the gold threads and go down towards the center, putting the needle exactly into the back of the previous stitch. To fill in tiny corners between circles where the linen shows, plunge one thread of gold to the reverse side with a tapestry needle and work with the remaining one, doubling it back on itself until the space is filled in.

Cover the entire fabric with pairs of couched circles, sometimes doubling back on the couched rows to fill the spaces completely (Diagram 3). Plunge thread to the reverse side with a large tapestry needle *afterwards* so that threads won't be caught up in the stitching on the reverse side.

To mount, cut out the exact shape of the band from crinoline or use your plastic pattern. Run a double gathering thread around the edges of the finished gold design. Place crinoline or plastic on the reverse side, draw up the gathering thread around it so that the turnbacks lie flat, and lightly glue them in place. If you wish, make piping from gold jersey fabric, lay it around the edges, and glue. Lay the gold chain down on the reverse side and sew it in place at the center and at both sides.

Cut suede cloth backing slightly larger than the finished band and glue it in place. When it is dry, trim the fabric flush against the band all around.

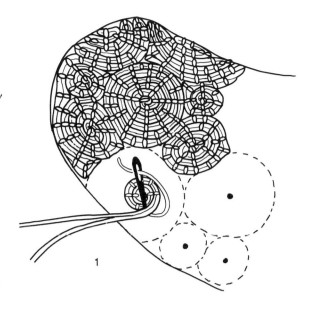

1

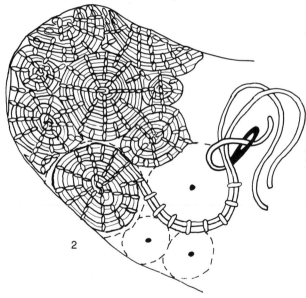

2

3

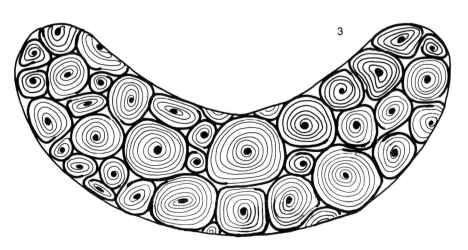

(Color photo, page 6.)

SHOPPING LIST
square (approximately 10")
  #14 interlock canvas
gold silk or cotton floss
Japanese gold thread
Maltese sewing silk ("horsetail")
yellow felt
10 (½"-diameter) domed
  brass buttons
button thread
heavy metallic gold cord
lightweight plastic
  (as used for file folders)
all-purpose glue
gold kid or silk fabric
gold chain

ECUADOR GOLD MEDALLION

Adapted from a prehistoric Inca nose ring, this design makes a beautiful pendant, pin, handbag clasp, or even a belt buckle similar to the one shown on page 112.

Using a permanent marker, trace the full-size pattern on canvas. Mount the canvas in an embroidery frame and, following the chart, work the stitches in alphabetical order.

A. Using two strands of floss, work the background in tent stitch (shaded areas on chart). Do not work over dots.
B. Couch one strand of Japanese gold with silk thread to fill circles. Work from the center out, leaving the dot open.
C. Pad each section of the shell with three layers of felt (see page 74). Couch Japanese gold on top, starting at the outer edge of the central motif and working towards the middle. Repeat for each segment. D. Using pointed scissors, pierce holes in the canvas large enough for a button shank to pass through. Secure buttons by knotting them to each other on the reverse side. E. Couch two strands of Japanese gold around the edge, covering needlepoint as necessary to make a smooth outline. F. Couch heavy cord next to Japanese gold, outlining lower circles as in the diagram.

To mount, trace a paper pattern from the outline on this page. Use it to cut out two identical pieces from plastic. Trim needlepoint, allowing ⅜" seam allowances. To eliminate bulk on the reverse side and make smooth curves, notch the canvas with small V-shaped cuts all around and glue it to one piece of plastic. Cover the second piece of plastic with gold kid or silk backing in the same manner and tape an upholstery weight to the reverse side. Stitch the two pieces together and couch Japanese gold around the edge to cover any bare canvas.

Secure the ends of a chain or cord to the tips of the wings with tiny stitches to make a pendant. For a handbag clasp such as the one shown on page 84, insert a tongue of fabric at the top center of the design as you stitch the back and front together. This forms a hinge that can be attached to the handbag. Then hooks, snaps, or a button can be added.

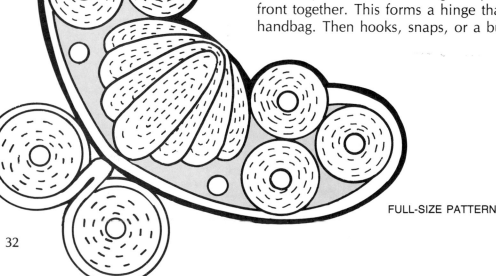

FULL-SIZE PATTERN

32

GOLD RIBBON RUFF

Wide gold ribbon makes today's version of an Elizabethan ruff. Make it from any ribbon—gold, silver, or colored silk.

Pin and baste the ribbon under and over as shown. Cut the ribbon when the ruff measures approximately 14½". Then sew the ruff to the narrow ribbon or cord with running stitches (Diagram 1).

Now make three flowers to attach to one end of the ribbon so that when the ruff is tied at the neck, the flowers will be centered. Cut one piece of ribbon 6" long, one 8½" long, and one 13½" long, and run a double row of gathering thread along the lower edge of each piece. Seam them as shown (Diagram 2).

Gather each flower at its base (Diagram 3) and attach all three in a cluster to one end of the ribbon.

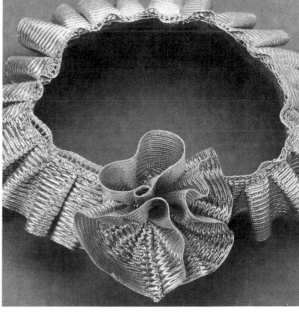

(Color photo, page 7.)

SHOPPING LIST
3 yards (1½"-wide) ribbon
1 yard gold cord or
  (⅜"-wide) ribbon
nylon sewing thread

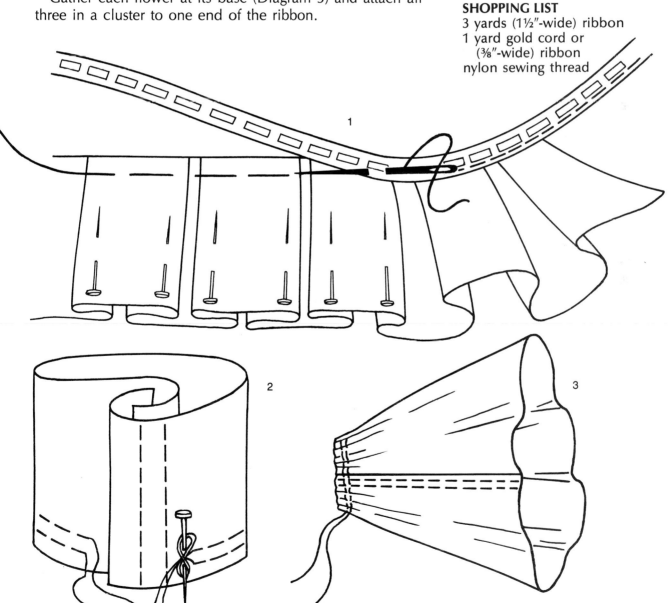

(Color photo, page 5.)

SHOPPING LIST
squares of gold felt
green cotton floss
#6 crewel needle
Japanese gold thread
all-purpose glue
leather fabric with jersey backing
plastic drinking straw or
 tube-shaped gold beads
nylon thread
lapis and jasper beads
necklace clasp

CHAPLET OF LEAVES

This necklace was inspired by the chaplet of leaves made in the Royal Sumerian workshops at Ur in Mesopotamia, centuries before Christ. The leaves could be made in any size and strung on cords instead of with the square-cut semi-precious stones shown here.

Outline the full-size leaf shape on felt for as many leaves as you require. Mount the felt in an embroidery frame. Using two strands of green cotton floss in a #6 crewel needle, couch a double strand of Japanese gold around the outline of the leaf, placing couching stitches on lines drawn as veins. Work round and round, couching rows close together until the leaf is covered. (Diagram 1.)

When couching is complete, plunge gold threads down through the fabric in the center, using a large tapestry or chenille needle (Diagram 2). On the reverse side, trim the ends ¼" long.

Cut out and glue finished leaf to a square of leather fabric. To glue, moisten both surfaces to be joined. Allow them to dry, and then remoisten one side. Press the layers together and, when dry, trim leather close against the edge.

Fold the end of each leaf over to the reverse side, placing small pieces of a drinking straw or tube-shaped beads inside the fold, and glue in place (Diagram 3). Thread the beads on nylon thread, interspersing leaves between them. Attach the necklace clasp.

FULL-SIZE
PATTERN

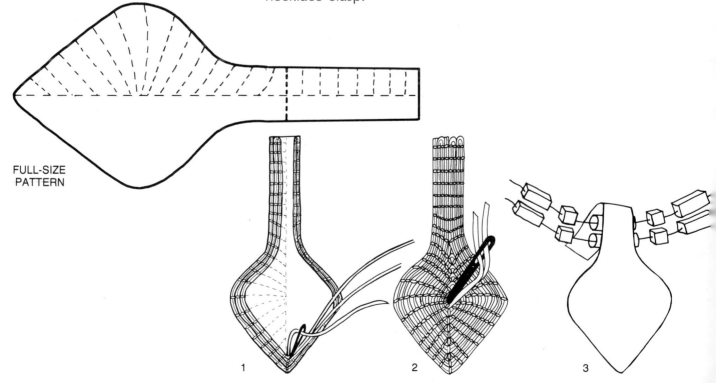

1   2   3

BUTTERFLY AND ROSE PENDANTS

Both of these pendants may be made with the self-covering button kits available at the notions counter. (You can also cut circles from the sort of lightweight plastic used in making file folders.) They may be hung on any kind of cord (see page 116) or attached to a store-bought choker. The rose is done by taking an existing fabric and outlining its pattern with gold buttonhole stitch. The butterfly is done in long and short shaded stitches outlined with gold on black satin. Follow the colors in the photograph on page 13 or use your own color scheme.

ROSE PENDANT

Choose any suitable small print design and outline it with open buttonhole stitch, using one strand of fine gold thread. Mount in the same way as the butterfly.

SHOPPING LIST
printed fabric
DMC Fil d'Or thread
self-covering button kit

BUTTERFLY PENDANT

Trace the butterfly, applying the design to fabric with white dressmaker's carbon. Mount the fabric in an embroidery hoop. Work wings in long and short stitch and circles in satin stitch. Outline the wings and fill the body with couched Japanese gold. Leave two gold strands loose with knotted ends for antennae.

Cover the button according to package directions. Note that the drawing is larger than the back of the button to allow for the domed surface.

If you prefer to cover plastic, cut two circles from it in the size required. Run a double row of gathering stitches around the outer edge of the finished needlework, trim ¼" beyond the gathering, and draw the gathering threads tightly over the plastic. Repeat this procedure to cover the second piece of plastic with plain fabric for the backing. Glue the two covered discs together. Stitch and edge with cord.

SHOPPING LIST
black satin fabric
white dressmaker's carbon
cotton floss
Japanese gold thread
1 (2½"-diameter) dome-topped
   self-covering button kit

(Color photos, page 13.)

FULL-SIZE PATTERN

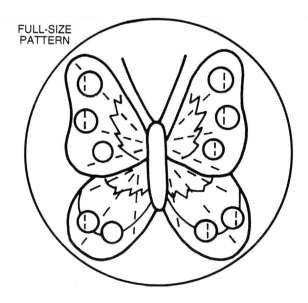

(Color photo, page 3.)

DOGWOOD BLOSSOMS

SHOPPING LIST
½ yard organdy
DMC Fil d'Or thread
white quilting thread
Pellon® or crinoline for backing
rhinestones by the yard
flat gold ribbon or braid

These organdy flowers were inspired by a magnificent Italian necklace made of rock crystal with blue diamond centers. The combination of organdy, gold thread, and rhinestones gives you a spray of blossoms that may be used as an unusual necklace or a hairband, or can even be stitched along the top of a wedding dress, with a matching garland for a wedding veil.

Put two thicknesses of organdy in an embroidery frame. Trace the outlines of flowers with Trace Erase™ marker. Work chain stitch around the border of each petal, using a #6 crewel needle and three strands of Fil d'Or thread (Diagram 1). Trim excess organdy away from each edge, cutting close to the chain stitch.

Gather the circle in the center with white quilting thread (Diagram 2), making two close rows of gathering stitches for better control. If you wish, push a tiny pad of cotton up into the middle of the gathered circle.

Mount Pellon® or crinoline fabric in an embroidery hoop. Lay the flower, right side up, on top and sew five or six rhinestones around the gathered center, working through both layers of fabric (Diagram 3). On the reverse side, cut away all but a small circle of the backing fabric; using this circle, attach the flowers to the cord (Diagram 4). You can use narrow gold ribbon or braid, grouping the larger flowers in the center and the smaller ones at the ends, overlapping them slightly so that the petals stand up.

FULL-SIZE PATTERNS

37

STAINED GLASS MEDALLIONS

SHOPPING LIST
40-mesh gauze or fine silk fabric
cotton floss or Au Vera Soie
cotton fabric for backing
lightweight plastic (as used for
    file folders)
upholstery weight
quilting batting
masking tape
fine macrame cord (optional)

Using silk or cotton floss, you can make medallions with the look of stained glass or enamel. Work on gauze for the pansy or tulip designs and on fine silk fabric for the lily of the valley. Add hangers of macrame, twisted cords, or rattail cord.

Stretch the background fabric in an embroidery hoop and trace either of the full-size designs on this page onto the fabric. Using two threads of floss on the silk or four threads on the gauze, work the entire design in satin stitch, angling the stitches as in the photograph. On the gauze, work the satin stitches side by side into every hole of the mesh, adding details such as bullion knot pansy centers on top afterwards.

Cut plastic to the exact pattern shape, attaching an upholstery weight and batting to the front with masking tape. Sew backing and completed design together, right sides facing, leaving an opening at the base. Turn right side out, slip in the plastic stiffener, and slip stitch the opening closed.

Measure a length of fine cord or floss long enough to surround the medallion and make a knotted macrame hanger all in one. Wrap six fine cords or six whole strands of cotton floss (36 threads) with one whole strand of floss. Begin at the center, wrapping enough cord or floss to surround the medallion as in the photograph. Then knot the cords on either side, following the macrame instructions on page 22. Center and attach the pendant with invisible stitches. Make a loop and button closing (see crochet button, page 143).

FULL-SIZE PATTERNS

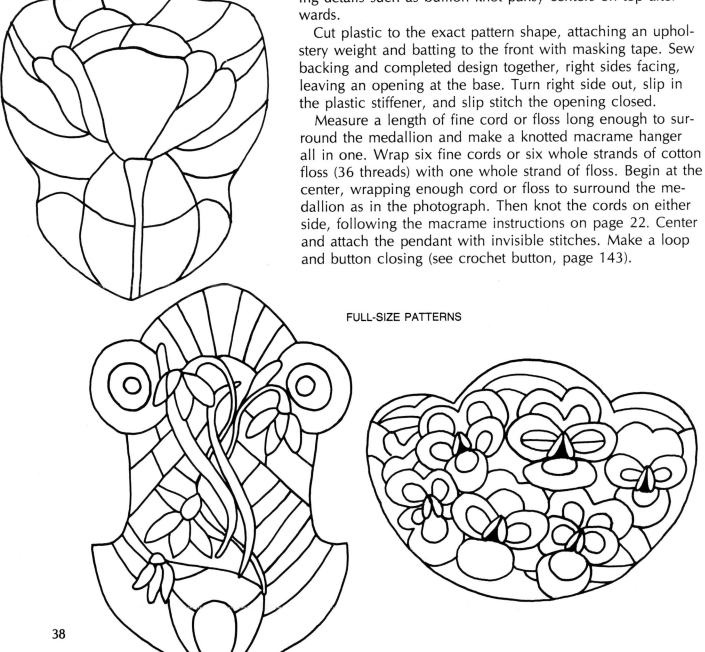

Flowering Garden Jewel Cabinet and Zippered Travelling Jewel Case are the ideal places to store your handmade jewels.

Painting the fabric.

Adding embroidery stitches.

Quilting around the outlines.

NEEDLEWORK TO WEAR   41

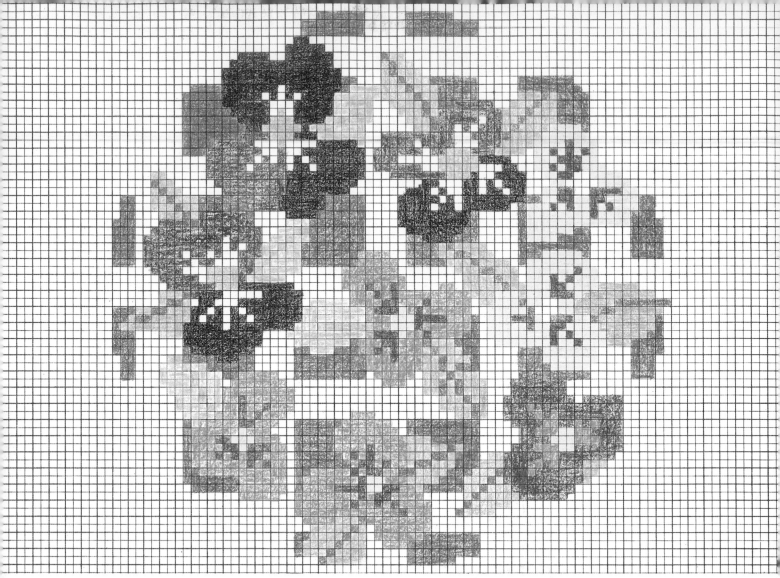

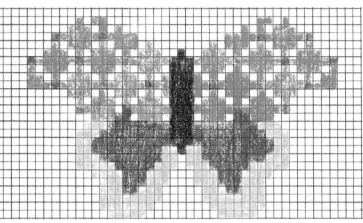

ZIPPERED TRAVELLING JEWEL CASE

Both the jewel cabinet shown on page 40 and the travelling jewel case here can be done either in cross-stitch or with acrylic paints. To cross-stitch the travel case, follow these instructions; to paint it, read about the jewel cabinet on the next page.

Mark a circle 5" in diameter on Aida cloth. Baste intersecting lines across the top to mark the center. Using two strands of cotton floss, work the cross-stitch design, counting from the chart opposite. Each square equals one cross-stitch.

To make the small butterfly that sits atop the case (also used as a closing for the jewel cabinet), cross-stitch the design and cut out, leaving ¼" all around for turnbacks. Sew the cotton batiste backing and the completed design together, right sides facing, leaving an opening through which to turn the design. Clip and notch turnbacks (Diagram 1) before turning right side out. Slide in twist-tie stiffener (dotted lines on Diagram 2) and invisibly stitch in position. Slip stitch opening closed (Diagram 2).

Wrap twist-ties, pipe cleaners, or metal-core candlewicking with blue cotton floss (Diagrams 3 and 4) and attach to the head for antennae. Stitch the butterfly in position on top of cross-stitched circle. For mounting and finishing, see page 151.

SHOPPING LIST
14-count Aida cloth
DMC cotton floss
blue cotton batiste
twist-ties, pipe cleaners, or
  metal-core candlewicking
silk fabric for mounting and lining
quilting batting
1 (16"-long) zipper

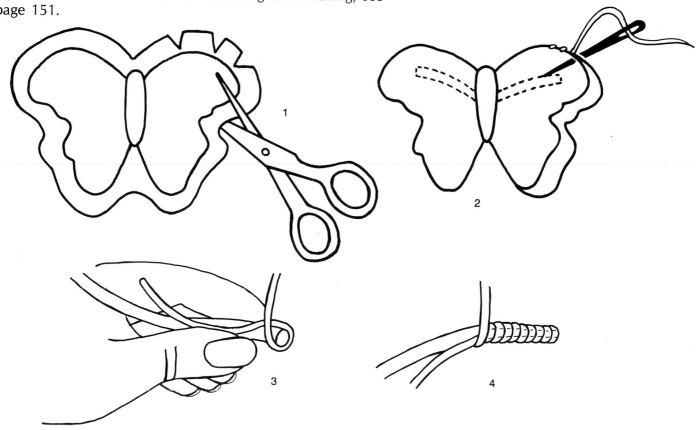

(Color photo, page 40.)

FLOWERING GARDEN JEWEL CABINET

To store your handmade jewels, make this updated translation of the magnificent antique boxes used by English gentlewomen.

Thanks to today's acrylic paint (see Suppliers) which dries permanently on fabric, you can paint your design in any color scheme of your choosing, add touches of embroidery, and finally quilt the whole thing to give it texture and dimension. The design is also attractive in cross-stitch.

The painting technique can also be used to make an attractive vest or jacket. To paint the box, follow these simple instructions. Mount your fabric on stretcher strips. Enlarge the pattern and trace it onto the fabric. Paint the design, allowing each color to dry before proceeding to the next. Acrylic paints are normally the right consistency just as they come; if necessary, you can thin them slightly with water.

When dry, outline the shapes with embroidery stitches as shown in the photograph. First stitch the centers of the flowers and leaves with six strands of floss. Then baste one layer of batting and one layer of muslin behind the finished design. With a stem stitch and two strands of floss, go around each flower, stitching through the batting and the muslin backing. Then, with a quilting backstitch and quilting thread, quilt around the white fence and trellis.

To cross-stitch the design, trace the pattern outlines onto Aida cloth and fill each each area with cross-stitch.

For mounting and finishing, see page 150.

SHOPPING LIST
Embroidery floss
1 (20" × 30") piece of heavy
   cardboard or illustration board
1 yard of cotton for lining
2 (1½") large covered hooks
   and eyes
staple gun

For a painted box:
   1 yard white cotton or
      polyester-cotton fabric
   artists' stretcher strips
   acrylic paints (tubes or liquid)
   1 yard muslin
   quilting batting
   quilting thread

For a cross-stitch box:
   1 yard 14-count
      Aida cloth

A—CUT 1

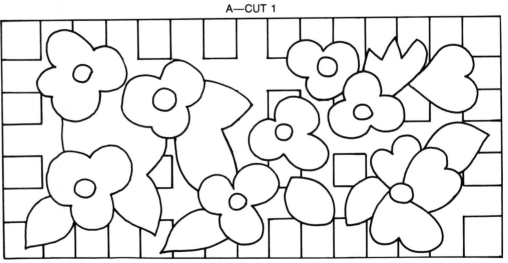

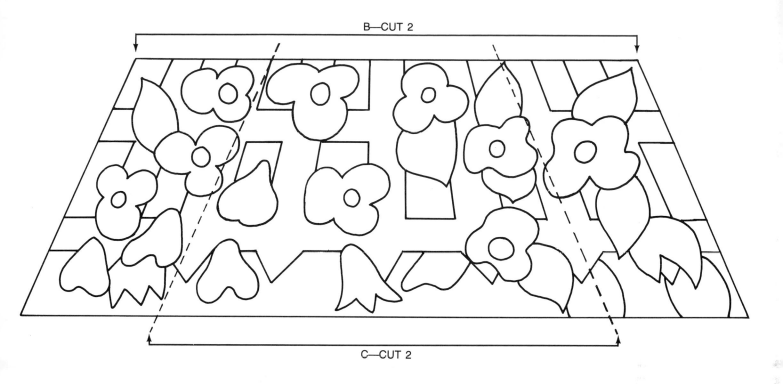

B—CUT 2

C—CUT 2

JOIN D & E TO MAKE F—CUT 2

D—CUT 2

E—CUT 2

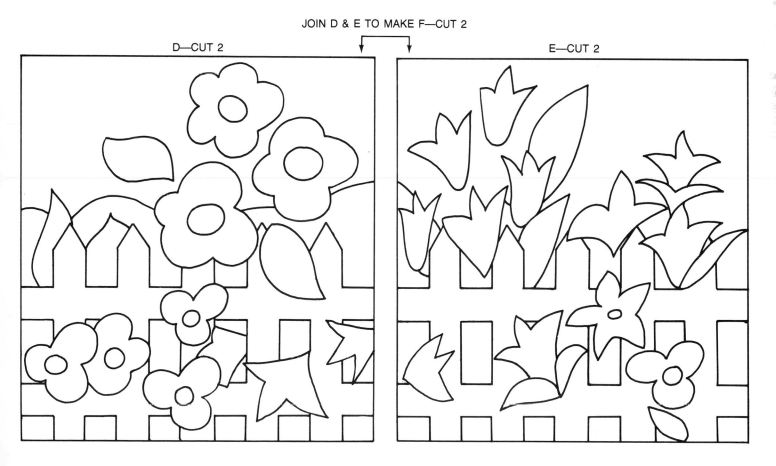

CLOTHING

One-of-a-kind designer clothes are excitingly different. More often than not, the thing that sets them apart is exquisite handwork. With a little practice, your obedient needle can be trained to produce all kinds of unique creations that are made just for you.

On the next pages you will find ideas for smocking, needlemade lace, couched gold evening wear, embroidered silk, quilted jackets and decorated sweaters. Once you are familiar with some of these kinds of needlework, you can enjoy creating all kinds of clothing without being an *haute couture* designer—the techniques themselves will set the styles for you. Fashion design today is more involved with needlework than ever before, so once you become aware, you will find inspiration everywhere.

Take lace, for instance. Nearly everyone has a cherished piece of it tucked away somewhere—a small scrap of an ancestor's christening robe, a filmy swatch you picked up in a thrift shop, your own wedding veil! At one time, lace was such an expensive luxury that noblemen were known to sell acres of land in order to afford it. A French courtier of 1630 boasted that he wore thirty-two acres of the best vineyard around his neck. Then came the sewing machine, invented expressly for duplicating handmade laces. What a paradox that this same machine later put us into unadorned, "strait-laced" clothes! But not for long. Now that lace is being appreciated once more, you could duplicate the blouse opposite. Embroider the center medallion, add your own pieces of machine or handmade lace, and you've created an heirloom.

The skirt on the next page is part of a dress made for the Paris Exhibition of 1851. You could make panels for an evening skirt in its original padded satin stitch, or you could work the design of roses and forget-me-nots in cross-stitch.

And finally, on the subject of things to wear, consult the *Quick and Easy* chapter further on. You'll find ideas for all kinds of things you can whip up overnight to add pizzazz to your wardrobe.

Left: English dress in 1850. (ENGLISH COSTUME OF THE NINETEENTH CENTURY, 1929.)

Opposite: The author in an antique blouse. Create your own VICTORIAN LACE BLOUSE with buttonhole stitches on sheer organza.

Opposite: Taffeta embroidered in padded satin stitch and French knots. Adapted from the dress brought from the Paris Exhibition of 1851 by the author's great-grandmother. Above: VICTORIAN SKIRT design charted for counted cross-stitch.

Left and above: OLD ENGLISH SMOCK in coffee-colored linen with spider's web buttons.

Below: Wool jersey fabric is smocked with honeycomb stitch in SMOCKING WITH A DIFFERENCE.

Opposite: Gold thread couched over felt padding create the raised effect in the GOLD LEAF CAMISOLE.

Below: The SWIRLING WAVE VEST, another glittering example of couched gold threads.

Coloring the design for this *PAINTED AND QUILTED SILK JACKET* is as simple as finger painting in kindergarten.

RE-EMBROIDERED LACE and SPRING BOU-
QUETS FOR A BLOUSE turn simple blouses
into a special ones.

Opposite: The CUTWORK SAILOR COLLAR
and WISTERIA BRANCH YOKE add elegance
to a store-bought blouse or one you make
yourself.

Opposite: A RUFFLED CAMEO becomes the centerpiece of an all-white blouse.

Below: A TABARD TOP transforms a skirt into an attractive late-day costume.

Opposite: This POPCORN PULLOVER can be knitted in any combination of colors and made to match every item in your wardrobe.

Right: The short-sleeved COTTON BOBBLE SWEATER is decorated here with bullion knot roses and lazy daisy stitches.

Below: This RIBBON CABLE SWEATER can be woven with any ribbon that matches your mood.

(Color photo, page 61.)

SHOPPING LIST
Handwork Tapestries medium weight
   cotton yarn, 5 (6,6) balls
1 pair each knitting needles,
   sizes 5 and 6
crochet hook, size G

COTTON BOBBLE SWEATER

Instructions for this sweater are for women's size small, with changes for medium and large in parentheses. Actual bust measurements of the sweater will be 33″ (36″, 39″). As always, check gauge carefully; four stitches equal one inch.
BOBBLE: k 1 * sl st just knitted back to left needle; k 1 into st just slipped, repeat from * 2 times more, chain formed. With left needle, pick up back loop of st in which first k 1 was made. K 1, pass top st of ch over last st knitted.
PATTERN: Row 1: K 3 * make bobble, k 5, rep from * ending with k 3. Row 2: P. Row 3: K. Row 4: P. Row 5: K 6 * make bobble, k 5, rep from * ending with k 6. Row 6: P. Row 7: K. Row 8: P. Rep these 8 rows for pattern. Work all pieces for sweater in pattern stitch, being careful to keep pattern as established when inc and dec.
FRONT: With smaller needles, cast on 66(72,78) sts; work in k 1, p 1 ribbing for 2½″. Change to larger needles and work even in pattern until piece measures 12½″(13″, 13½″) or desired length to underarm.
SHAPE ARMHOLES: Bind off 3(3,4) sts at beg of next 2 rows. Dec 1 st each side every other row 2 times. Work even on 56 (62,66) sts until piece measures 5½″(6″, 6½″) from beg of armhole shaping.
SHAPE NECK: Work across 17(18,18) sts; join second ball of yarn; bind off 22(26,30) sts; work rem st. Working both sides tog, dec 1 st at each neck edge every row 5 times. At same time, when piece measures 7″(7½″, 8″) from armhole shaping, shape shoulders. Bind off 6 sts at shoulder edge 1 time; then 6(7,7) sts 1 time.
BACK: Work same as for front until piece measures 4″ above armhole shaping. Divide for back opening: Work 28 (31,33) sts; join new ball of yarn and work rem sts. Working both sides at same time, work even until piece measures 6½″(7″,7½″) from beg of armhole shaping. At each neck edge, bind off 14(16,18) sts, then dec 1 st each neck edge 2 times. At same time when piece measures 7″(8″, 8½″) from beg of armhole shaping, shape shoulders: Bind off 6 sts at shoulder edge 1 time; then 6(7,7) sts 1 time.
SLEEVE: With smaller needles, cast on 50(50,54) sts. Work in k 1, p 1 ribbing for 1½″, inc 10 sts evenly spaced across last ribbing row. Change to large needles and work even in pattern until piece measures 4½″(4½″, 5″).
SLEEVE CAP SHAPING: Bind off 3(3,4) sts at beg of next 2 rows. Dec 1 st each edge next row, then every other row until there are 34(34,36) sts left. Work even until cap of sleeve measures 5½″ (5½″, 6″) from beg cap shaping. Bind off.

FINISHING: Sew shoulder, underarm, and sleeve seams. Set in sleeves, gathering top to fit. With right side facing, work crochet neck edge: Row 1: Beginning at the bottom of the back opening, work 12 sc along left edge of back opening; work sc evenly spaced around neck; work 12 sc along right edge of back opening. Row 2: Sc in first 3 sc of row 1; (sc, ch 3, sl st into sc, picot sc made) in next sc; ch 3 for button loop, sk 2 sc; work 2 sc, then picot sc; ch 3 for second button loop; sk 2 sc, work 1 sc, then picot sc in corner; * sc in next 3 sc, work picot sc, rep from * around, end with sc in 12 sc along right edge. Lap left edge over right and sew tog at bottom of opening.
BUTTONS: Ch 2. Round 1: 5 sc in second ch from hook. Round 2: 2 sc in each sc (10 sc). Round 3: Sc in each sc around. Round 4: Stuff, work 2 tog around (5 sc). Sew shut and sew buttons in place.

RIBBON CABLE SWEATER

The special technique for working this sweater leaves spaces in the cables through which you can wind ribbons. Instructions are for small, with changes for medium and large in parentheses. The bust will measure 34" (36", 38"). Check gauge before starting; 5 stitches and 6 rows equal 1".
FRONT: With smaller needles, cast on 78 (84, 88) sts; work in k 1, p 1 ribbing for 2½". Inc 7 st evenly across last ribbing row. 85 (91, 95) st. Change to larger needles and work in cable pattern as follows.
CABLE: Row 1: k 7 (10, 12) * p 2, place 5 sts on dpn and hold at back of work, k 5, k the sts from dpn, p 2, k 5, repeat from * 3 times more ending last rep with k 7 (10, 12). Rows 2 through 8: k the k stitches and p the p stitches. Rep these 8 rows for pattern. Work even in pattern until piece measures 13½" from the beginning (or desired length to underarm).
ARMHOLE SHAPING: Continue working in pattern; bind off 4 (5, 6) sts at beg of next two rows; then dec 1 st on both sides every k row 2 (4, 4) times. Work even until 5½" (6", 6½") from beg of armhole shaping.
NECK SHAPING: Keeping to established pattern, work 26 (26, 27) sts, join a second ball of yarn, work 21 sts and place them on holder, work last 26 (26, 27) sts. Working each side with separate yarn, at each neck edge dec 1 st every row 6 times (20 (20, 21) st each side). Work in pattern until armhole measures 7½" (8", 8½").

(Color photo, page 61.)

SHOPPING LIST
Unger's Darling Yarn, 9 (9, 10) balls
knitting needles sizes, 6 and 8
double pointed needles, size 6

SHOULDER SHAPING: At each arm edge, bind off 5 sts 4 (4, 3) times, 6 sts 0 (0, 1) time.

BACK: Work same as front but omit cable pattern (plain stockinette). Omit neck shaping. When armhole measures 7½" (8", 8½"), shape shoulders same as for front. Place remaining 33 sts on holder.

SLEEVE: With smaller needles, cast on 41 (41, 43) sts. Work in k 1, p 1 ribbing for 2½". Change to larger needles and k across row, inc 10 sts evenly spaced. Work sleeve in St st, inc 1 st each side of row every ¾" until there are 75 (77, 79) sts. Work even until sleeve measures 17" from start (or desired length to underarm).

SHAPE SLEEVE CAP: Bind off 4 (5, 6) sts at beg of next 2 rows. Dec 1 st each edge next row, then every other row until 3" (3½", 4") above beginning of cap shaping. Bind off.

FINISHING: Sew shoulder and underarm seams. Sew sleeve seams. Sew in sleeves gathering top of sleeve to fit.

NECKBAND: With dpn from right side, beg at right shoulder seam, k across sts on holder at back of neck, pick up and k 1 st in each st and row on shaped neck edge, k sts from holder on front, pick up sts on shaped edge. Be sure to have even number of stitches. Join. Rib in k 1, p 1 for 1". With larger needle, bind off in ribbing stitch.

(Color photo, page 60.)

POPCORN PULLOVER

These instructions are for women's size small; changes for medium and large are in parentheses. Be sure to check your gauge and adjust needle size if necessary. Five stitches and six rows equal one inch. Finished bust measurement is 32" (34", 36"). Popcorns are 17 stitches apart with 13 rows between.

POPCORN PATTERN STITCH: Each popcorn (PO) is made by working a cluster of 5 sts into 1 st and working 4 rows of St st (k 1 row, p 1 row) over these 5 sts. Row 1: On right side k 2(5,7), place marker on needle, * drop A yarn and tie on length of B yarn. In next st, using B, k, p, k, p, k (5 sts worked in 1 st), turn work, p all 5 sts, turn, k all 5 sts, turn, p all 5 sts, turn, k all 5 sts, do not turn work. With left needle, pass the first 4 sts, one after the other, over the 5th st which remains on the needle—1 PO made. Drop the end of B yarn, do not cut, pick up A yarn, k 17 sts, rep from * 3 times, PO, place marker, k 2(5,7). Rows 2-12: Beg with p row, work even in St st, slipping markers. Row 13: k 11(14,16), * PO, k 17, rep from * twice, PO, k 11(14,16). Rows 14-24: Rep rows 2-12. These 24 rows form pat.

BACK: With smaller needles, using color A, cast on 77 (83,87)sts. Work in k 1, P 1 ribbing for 2". Change to larger needles. Work in St st for 4 rows. Next row: Rep the 24 rows of PO pat to 15" from beg or desired length to underarm, ending with p row.

Armholes: Keeping pat, at beg of next 2 rows, bind off 3(4,4) sts. Dec 1 st each side every 2nd row 3(4,5) times. Work even on 65(67,69) sts until armholes measure 7"(7½",8") from beg.

Shoulders: Bind off 6(7,7) sts at beg of next 4 rows, bind off 8(7,8) sts at the beg of next 2 rows. Place 25 sts for back of neck on holder.

FRONT: Work same as back until armholes measure 5"(5½",6"), ending with a P row.

Nec. K 24 (25,26) sts, place center 17 sts on holder, join a 2nd skein of yarn, k 24 (25, 26) sts. Working on each side with separate yarn, dec 1 st at each neck edge every 2nd row 4 times, 20 (21, 22) sts left on each shoulder shaping shoulders as on Back when armholes are the same length as back.

Then bind off the rem 8 (7,8) sts at beg of next row.

SLEEVES: With smaller needles and color A, cast on 41(41,43) sts. Work in k 1, p 1 rib for 2". Change to larger needles. Work in St st for 2 rows. Begin pat—Row 1: k 2 (2,3) sts, place marker, PO, k 17, PO, k 17, PO, place marker, k 2(2,3) sts. Rows 2-12: Beg with p row, work in St st slipping markers. Row 13: k 11(11,12), PO, k 17, PO, k 11(11,12). Row 14: P. Continue in pat, inc 1 st each side of this row and every ¾", 9(10,10) times more. When sufficient sts have been inc, add a new PO at each side. Work on 61(63-65) sts until sleeve measures 17" from beg.

Shape Sleeve Cap: Keeping in pat at beg of next 2 rows, bind off 3(4,4) sts. For large size only: Dec 1 st each side every 4th row once. For all sizes: Dec 1 st each side every 2 rows 14(16,16) times. For small size only: Dec 1 st each side every row twice. For all sizes: Dec 2 sts each side of next row. Bind off rem 19 sts.

FINISHING: Block pieces. Knot individual ends of B yarn on wrong side to secure PO's. If rounder PO is desired, *before* knotting ends, thread needle with end of B and run through first PO sts, gathering them up tightly to form a ball. Knot ends on wrong side of sweater. Weave shoulder seams. Sew underarm and sleeve seams. Sew in sleeves.

NECKBAND: With dpn from right side, beg at right shoulder seam, k across sts on holder at back of neck, pick up and k 1 st in each st and row on shaped neck edge, k sts from holder, pick up sts on shaped edge. Count sts and be sure to have an even number. Join. Rib in k 1, p 1 for 1 ". With larger needle, bind off in ribbing.

SHOPPING LIST
A. Unger's Darling Yarn 7(7,8) balls, 1-4/10 oz. balls, any color
B. Paternayan crewel wool (36", 3-ply), 2 oz. (approximately 140 strands) in desired colors
1 pair each knitting needles, sizes 7 and 8
1 set (4) double-pointed needles, size 6

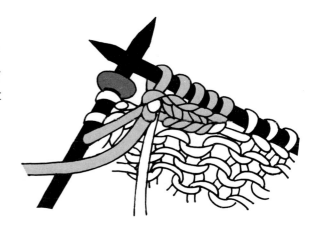

SPRING BOUQUETS FOR A BLOUSE

You can use the techniques shown here and on the following pages to decorate all kinds of blouses, whether you are making your own or buying one in a store. This blouse and the four that follow it are also available as "Almost Ready to Wear" kits (see page 154).

The Spring Bouquet is stitched with miniature bullion knots. Worked with two strands of cotton floss, the flowers add a delicate touch of color to an all-white blouse.

Trace the pattern from this page onto the finished blouse with a hard, sharp pencil. Scatter the flower sprigs as you prefer in an allover pattern. Begin and end off the embroidery for each sprig separately; do not jump from one to the other or the thread will show through from the reverse side. Work the stems in stem stitch and the leaves in lazy daisy stitch. Work the flower centers in short bullion knots (Diagram 4, opposite page). To make the longer, outer petals, add more twists to the needle, resulting in a curve.

FULL-SIZE
PATTERN

RE-EMBROIDERED LACE

Embroidery in cotton floss combines beautifully with lace, whether the design is white-on-white or has subtle touches of color added. First find lace with a pattern that can be easily cut into separate sections, such as the floral design shown here. Carefully cut around the reinforced edges, arrange the cutout pieces of lace in a pleasing design on your blouse front, and baste each piece in place (Diagram 1). Appliqué the lace by machine, using overlock stitch, or by hand, using buttonhole (Diagram 2), Point de Paris, or Point Turc stitches. When stitching is complete, carefully trim away the blouse fabric that lies behind the lace, cutting close against the appliqué edge (Diagram 3).

Now you are ready to add the embroidery. If the design calls for it, you can add stems, leaves, or a bow to connect the motifs. Highlight the lace with stitches such as padded satin stitch, french knots, bullion knots, and stem stitch, working as much or as little as you prefer. Begin and end off with small, invisible stitches, remembering that everything that happens on the reverse will show through to the front.

(Color photo, page 56.)

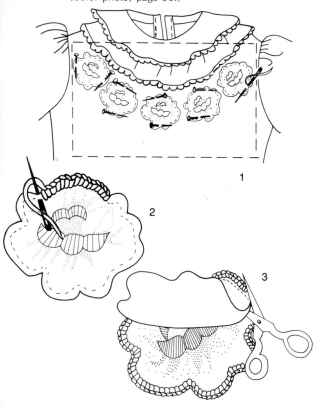

RUFFLED CAMEO

This oval cameo with a flower basket or a cornucopia design can be embroided with cotton floss, edged with lace, and used to accent a high-collared blouse.

Trace full-size design on polyester-cotton batiste and mount the fabric in an embroidery frame. Follow the guide below to work the stitches, using one strand of cotton floss. Work the cornucopia in split stitch, the basket in cross bars. (See Laid Work Diagrams 4, 5, and 6, page 147.)

Cut a square of batiste for a lining. Stitch it to the finished embroidery, right sides facing, leaving a small opening at the bottom. Trim edges down to a ¼" seam allowance and snip all curved edges up to stitching. Turn right side out, stitch opening closed, and press flat with a warm iron.

Join the ends of the lace to form a circle and gather by placing two parallel lines of running stitches on one edge. Adjust gathers and pin the cameo outside the lines of stitching. Stitch in place. Pin the cameo in the desired location on the blouse and slip stitch it in place from the reverse side.

(Color photo, page 58.)

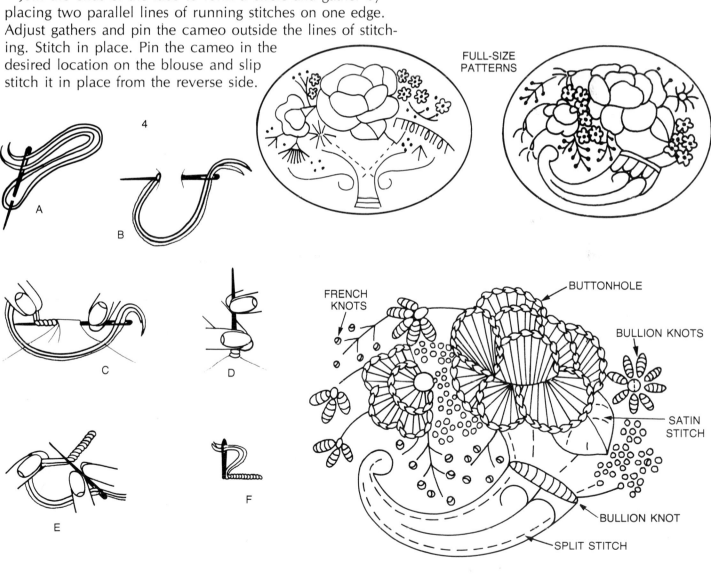

CUTWORK SAILOR COLLAR

The dramatic effect of cutwork is shown when you remove parts of the background after the stitching is complete. The design is a bolder version of the organza collar shown on page 111, and is worked entirely in one stitch: buttonhole. Because it is done through two layers of fabric, this cutwork design can be used to ornament any favorite blouse.

Trace the full-size design here and position it on your blouse. With two strands of cotton floss, work running stitches on the inner edge of the frame on the design (broken lines on pattern). Work buttonhole stitch (Diagram 1) all around, loops to the inside, working *over* the running stitch and through both layers of fabric. Next work the rose and the leaves in the same way, but with loops to the outside of each shape.

As you come to each bar connecting the design to the outer border, throw the thread across and take one stitch into the border; go back and take a stitch into the last buttonhole stitch you worked and go back to the border again. This will give you a foundation bar of three threads. Buttonhole over these threads *without going through the fabric,* covering the bar with closely packed, even stitches (Diagram 2). Secure the thread into your previous buttonhole stitch when you come to the end of the bar and continue buttonholing around the rose or leaf, working once again into the fabric.

To cut fabric away when all the stitching is complete, carefully pierce the fabric with small, pointed scissors in the centers of toned areas shown on the pattern. Make a slit towards the corner and cut fabric away close to the buttonhole loops (Diagram 3). Carefully cut fabric away from behind the buttonholed bars until all the fabric shown by shaded areas on the pattern has been removed.

FULL-SIZE PATTERN

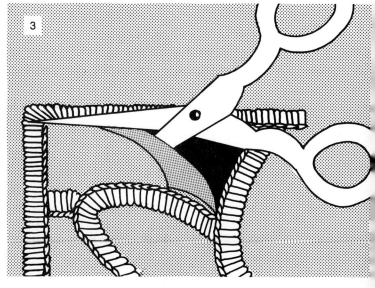

WISTERIA BRANCH YOKE

This delicate curving design would be equally attractive on a collar, a blouse front, the yoke of a dress, or a blouse as shown here.

Trace the half-design shown onto folded tracing paper; flip over the paper and trace the other half.

Mount the fabric in a frame. Transfer the complete design, using the center fold of the tracing paper to help you center the design. Using one thread of floss, embroider the stitches. Work the branches in stem stitch and the flowers and leaves in satin stitch, slanting the stitches. Use padded satin stitch for small buds to make clear-cut shapes. Outline larger petals with split stitch first to make crisp edges.

(Color photo, page 57.)

HALF OF
FULL-SIZE
PATTERN

CENTER FOLD

(Color photo, page 47.)

SHOPPING LIST
½ yard champagne or
flesh-colored organza
cotton floss
vinyl shelf paper (optional)
approximately 30 yards of
champagne lace (optional)

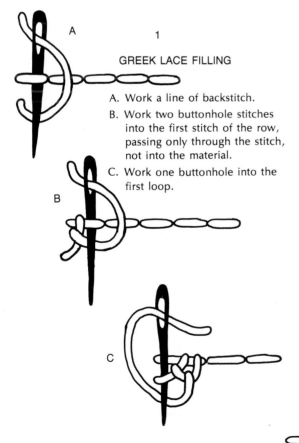

1

GREEK LACE FILLING

A. Work a line of backstitch.

B. Work two buttonhole stitches
into the first stitch of the row,
passing only through the stitch,
not into the material.

C. Work one buttonhole into the
first loop.

VICTORIAN LACE BLOUSE

Punto In Aria, literally, "a stitch in the air," is the name given to the beautiful Italian needlemade lace from which this blouse orginates. You can duplicate the center medallion in buttonhole stitch on sheer organza and surround it with a patchwork of frothy champagne lace. Alternatively, work the medallion as the focal point of an organza or silk blouse.

To embroider the medallion, outline the full-size design on silk organza with a Trace Erase™ pen. Using two threads of floss in a blunt tapestry needle, work Greek lace filling (Diagram 1) over the areas shown in gray on the chart. Begin each block with a row of backstitches along the length of each section, signified by the bold dotted lines on the chart. Work the Greek lace filling into this backstitch. Note that the needle only passes through the fabric at the ends of each line. Space the blocks of stitches apart to form an openwork effect. To achieve this, you may find it necessary to occasionally work into every other backstitch instead of every one on the first row. When each area is complete, stretch out the network and hold it in position with a small stitch on each bar along the base of the design.

Next, work the spiders' webs (Diagrams 2 and 3). Then work the buttonhole stitch, holding a bundle of threads under the buttonhole stitching to pad it as you work (Diagram 4).

Trim the organza away from the outside edges of the medallion and set your finished embroidery in the yoke of any blouse or enlarge the separate yoke pattern shown here (Diagram 5), following the method described for the re-embroidered lace on page 66. You can convert any blouse into a Victorian one by setting the medallion into this "V" shaped separate yoke. Fastened with buttons at the shoulders and edged with lace, it can be worn over a plain blouse of the same color with great effect.

Alternatively, make a crazy quilt of antique lace to surround your embroidery. Outline the pattern for your blouse front on vinyl shelf paper. (The vinyl gives you a firm surface for working and the needle glances off the shiny surface so that the stitching cannot catch.) Pin the lace in place and secure each piece to the next with Point de Paris stitches (page 125). When your stitching is complete, simply clip the basting stitches and lift the finished lace off the paper. Use this procedure to make each pattern piece from lace. Finish the high collar and the cuffs with a gathered ruffle of lace.

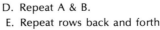

D. Repeat A & B.

E. Repeat rows back and forth
to form an openwork
mesh.

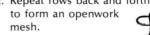

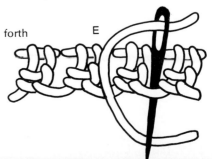

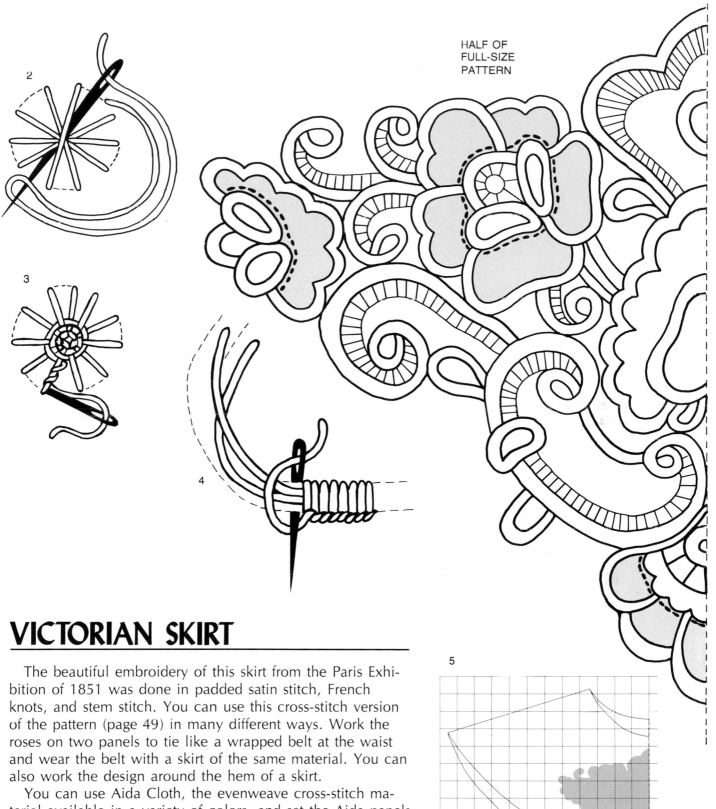

VICTORIAN SKIRT

The beautiful embroidery of this skirt from the Paris Exhibition of 1851 was done in padded satin stitch, French knots, and stem stitch. You can use this cross-stitch version of the pattern (page 49) in many different ways. Work the roses on two panels to tie like a wrapped belt at the waist and wear the belt with a skirt of the same material. You can also work the design around the hem of a skirt.

You can use Aida Cloth, the evenweave cross-stitch material available in a variety of colors, and set the Aida panels into a skirt of another fabric. Another alternative is to baste waste canvas onto silk. You then count the stitches from the graph, working right through the canvas and the fabric. When the stitching is complete, carefully pull out the canvas threads, leaving the design on the silk fabric.

(Color photo, page 54.)

SHOPPING LIST
silk fabric
commercial jacket pattern
paraffin wax
four stretcher strips
beeswax
denatured or ethyl alcohol
urea
baking soda
Procion dyes (see Suppliers)
paint brushes
newsprint or paper towels
quilting batting
lining fabric

PAINTED AND QUILTED SILK JACKET

The excitement of making clothes with quilting is in combining fabulous fabrics. The frustration of it, sometimes, is finding the right print in that perfect color. The solution: create your own! You will discover a whole new world when you combine fabric painting with quilting and embroidery—and you'll find that it's as easy as painting in kindergarten!

The jacket shown here is made in pure silk painted with Procion dyes to give the effect of watercolor. Parallel horizontal rows of machine or hand quilting keep it crisp and tailored, but light as a feather.

Fit your paper jacket pattern, making any necessary adjustments. Outline each pattern piece onto the silk fabric with basting stitches. Staple the first piece of marked fabric onto stretcher strips and pull taut.

(Note: Because this project involves the use of hot wax, which is flammable, and dyes, which are poisonous, please be very careful, especially if you have small children in the house.)

Melt equal quantities of beeswax and paraffin in a double boiler. When hot (not smoking, but freeflowing), paint the outlines of the design (page 149) on your fabric freehand or by following a drawing placed beneath so that you can see through (Diagram 1). Take care to connect lines so that the silhouette shapes are self-contained, because this wax outline will prevent your colors from running into each other

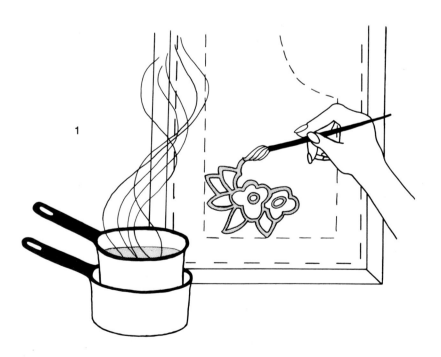

1

just like a stencil. Reverse the fabric to paint on the other side to ensure complete coverage. Let the wax dry.

Now mix your dyes. In a glass container, mix ½ cup of water, ½ cup of denatured or ethyl alcohol, one tablespoon of urea, and ½ to ⅔ of a teaspoon of baking soda.

Put a small quantity of the dye powder into a smaller glass container and add the liquid mixture a little at a time until the desired shade is achieved. Repeat for each color.

Paint colors on evenly; do not load the brush too heavily (Diagram 2). The dye will run easily to coat both sides of the fabric, so you won't be able to tell the right side from the wrong side. It will also run into another color if you have not coated the outlines sufficiently with wax. Sometimes, the blended effect may be desired. In this case, hasten the drying by adding more alcohol and less water to the mixture to obtain a watercolor effect of pale shades with a misty blur between each. Special effects can be obtained by sprinkling salt on the finished, but still damp, painting. This will bleach it in speckles. The addition of embroidery can be really beautiful, adding texture to the design, but is not necessary.

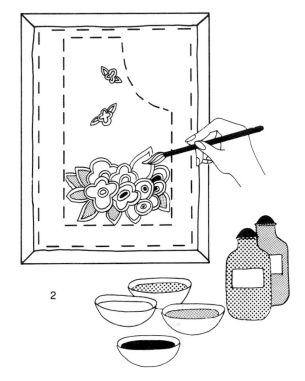

2

When you have finished painting and the fabric is dry, cover the ironing board with a thick layer of newsprint. (This is available unprinted at art supply stores. You can also use old newspapers covered with a layer of paper towels.) Put the fabric on top of the paper and put another thick layer of newsprint on top. Press with a hot iron so that the wax melts and runs into the paper (Diagram 3). Your design will appear with white lines between each color.

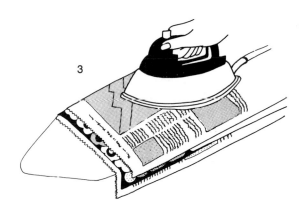

3

Now make the design permanent. Sandwich each piece of fabric between layers of paper towels and roll it loosely, taking care that dyed surfaces do not touch one another. Steam this roll in a double boiler or pressure cooker to set dye; do not allow fabric to touch water or it will run.

Cut a rectangle around each pattern piece of fabric and prepare for quilting by layering it with batting and lining fabric. Stitch in parallel horizontal lines by hand or machine (Diagram 4). A seam guide will help keep lines straight.

When quilting is complete, trim each piece with ¼" turnbacks. To assemble, blind stitch the side and shoulder seams, right sides facing, and then set in the sleeves. Clean finish by edging with silk bias binding.

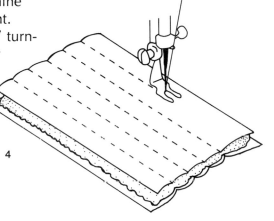

4

(Color photo, page 52.)

SHOPPING LIST
commercial camisole pattern
satin, velvet, or silk fabric
yellow felt
Japanese gold thread
Maltese sewing silk ("horsetail")
string (optional)

GOLD LEAF CAMISOLE

A glamorous evening top can be made with a design of raised gold leaves. The repoussé effect is achieved by padding with layers of felt and couching gold thread on top.

Start by pinning together and fitting your paper pattern, making any necessary adjustments. Lay the pattern pieces on the fabric, leaving free a clear rectangle of fabric around the front panel so it can be mounted on stretcher strips.

Mark the outline and the center front line of the front panel with basting stitches and transfer the leaf pattern here, matching up the center lines on the pattern to the basting line on the fabric. Mount the fabric on the stretcher strips.

To pad each leaf, cut three leaves from yellow felt, making each one slightly smaller than the other. Sew the smallest of the three to the center of the leaf shape you have marked on the fabric, securing it all around with tiny stitches at right angles to the edge. Keep these stitches close together to prevent the edges from puckering. Layer the medium-sized leaf on top and secure it in the same manner, and then finish by stitching the largest leaf in place. You will have a smooth, raised surface that is high at the center and contoured at the sides (Diagram 1).

Now couch the gold thread closely over the felt. With one strand of waxed horsetail, couch one thread of gold around the leaf, starting at the outside and working towards the center. Work the branches by couching a single strand of gold between each spray of leaves (Diagram 2).

Assemble the camisole according to pattern instructions. If your pattern calls for narrow straps, try this simple method. Cut a 4" × 18" piece of bias fabric. Fold it in half lengthwise, right sides together, and enclose a 19" piece of string in the fold. Secure the string at one end. Machine stitch alongside the string. Trim ¼" beyond the stitched line. Turn right side out by pulling the string; then trim the end to free and dispose of the string.

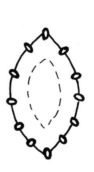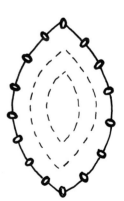

1

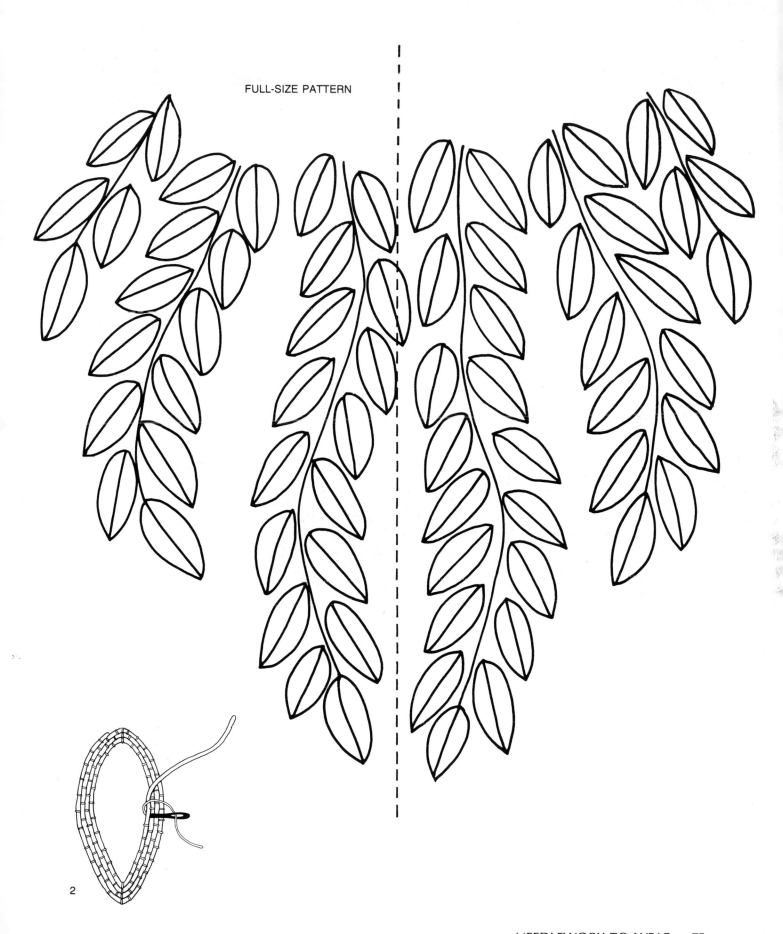

FULL-SIZE PATTERN

2

(Color photo, page 53.)

SHOPPING LIST
commercial vest pattern
mock suede fabric
Japanese gold thread
Maltese sewing silk ("horsetail")
beeswax
sequins

SWIRLING WAVE SUEDE VEST

With sequins scattered like foam at the crest of the waves, this design has a regal effect when worked in gold on red mock suede. It would be equally striking in white silk on black velvet or in brown floss combined with beadwork on chamois leather.

Outline your pattern pieces for the two fronts on fabric with basting stitches. Using the photograph as a guide, trace the individual swirl motifs in a pleasing arrangement on the vest and mount the fabric on stretcher strips or in an embroidery frame. Using waxed silk thread, couch two strands of gold thread on all of the outlines. Begin each swirl with doubled gold and end it by plunging the threads one at a time to the backside (Diagram 1). Sew down sequins where indicated (Diagram 2).

Line and assemble the vest according to the instructions given on your pattern.

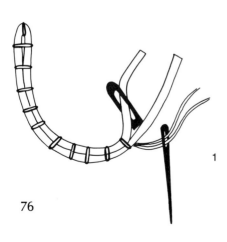

1

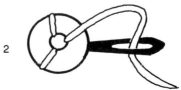

2

76

TABARD TOP

A tabard top made from two decorative rectangles of fabric can be attached to a skirt or be worn separately. Either way, it can convert a simple skirt into a lovely costume.

Make the tabard from two rectangles or curve the lower edges in a shield shape. Either way, use graph paper to cut out a correctly sized pattern before you start. Average finished size is 10" x 12". Stretch fabric in an embroidery frame and outline the design with a Trace Erase™ pen. Using two threads of silk floss, stitch the flowers in long and short stitch, leaves in satin stitch, and centers in lattice filling. Pine branches are straight stitches radiating from center.

To surround the pattern with ribbons, tape the completed embroidery to a firm surface. Cut a 5¼" × 6½" rectangle of graph paper and center it over the design. Lightly glue ribbon around the paper, mitering corners. Cut another graph paper rectangle 7" × 8"; surround it with 1½"-wide ribbon or fabric. Borders can be edged with narrow contrasting ribbon for added effect. Bind edges with bias tape. Add shoulder straps of ribbon or fabric and ties for the sides.

(Color photo, page 59.)

SHOPPING LIST
1 yard silk fabric
Au Vera Soie or Ping Ling silk floss
graph paper
ribbons in various widths
all-purpose glue
bias tape

FULL-SIZE PATTERN

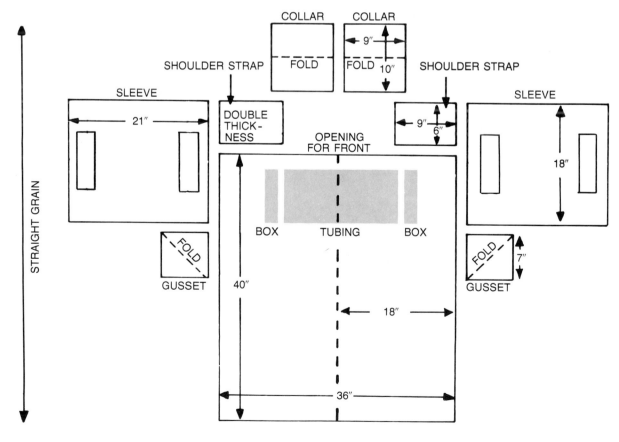

(Color photo, page 51.)

OLD ENGLISH SMOCK

In medieval times, smocking was to England what blue jeans are to America today. Farmers adopted the "smock frock" and each part of the country developed individual variations of the design. Each smock had feather-stitched patterns illustrating the occupation of its owner—woodsmen had trees and leaves, shepherds had crooks, and so on. All smocks were cut from square or oblong pieces of fabric and not a single curve was ever used, giving the garments a classic simplicity.

The smock shown here is made of coffee-colored linen and is cut from the old English pattern. Linen is the traditional fabric, but you can choose almost any fabric, from heavy cotton to wool challis, from jersey or lightweight silk to organza.

Follow the pattern here to make a paper pattern to use in cutting out the smock. The measurements given are for an average size and do not include seam allowances; adjustments can easily be made, since each piece is either square or rectangular. To ensure a perfect fit, pin the paper pattern pieces together and try them on before cutting, folding in the fullness allowed for the smocking to one third the width of the sleeves, the front, and the back.

On your paper pattern, draw lines for the base of the boxes, or embroidered panels, and for the tubing, or smocked areas, at a level comfortable for you. (That level is generally in a line with the underarm seam.)

Unpin the pattern and lay it on the fabric to cut in the most economical way. You will need to cut one large rectangle for the back, four shoulder straps, and two of each of the remaining pattern pieces. Because the smock opens down the front like a coat, you will need to cut two rectangles, each half the width of the back, for the front. You will also need to cut two bands for the buttons and buttonholes, each 3" wide and the length of the front.

With a contrasting thread, baste around the areas you marked on the pattern for the boxes and the tubing, following the threads of the fabric. Prepare for the gathering within the tubing by marking evenly spaced spots on the reverse side. This can be done with commercial smocking spot transfers or by lining up a strip of canvas to cover the tubing area and running a pencil along every other row, across the width. The pencil marks penetrate to the fabric, leaving evenly spaced spots. Each row of spots must be lined up with the previous row so that, when drawn up, the gathers create the vertical folds known as reeds. Be sure that these reeds are truly vertical or your smock will hang crookedly.

When marking is done, transfer the pattern for the heart-shaped embroidery in the box (Diagram 1) and work it in feather stitch, using cotton floss. If you like, repeat the pattern in a smaller scale on the collar and shoulder straps.

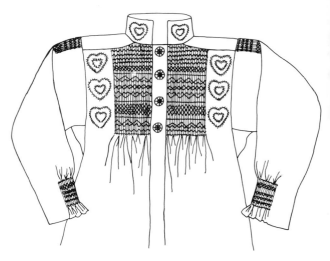

1

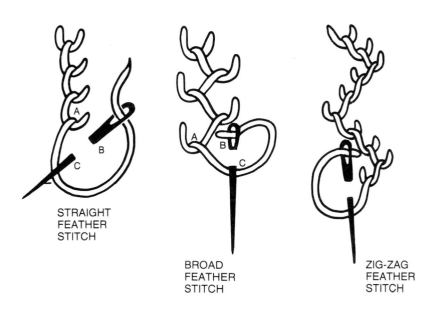

STRAIGHT
FEATHER
STITCH

BROAD
FEATHER
STITCH

ZIG-ZAG
FEATHER
STITCH

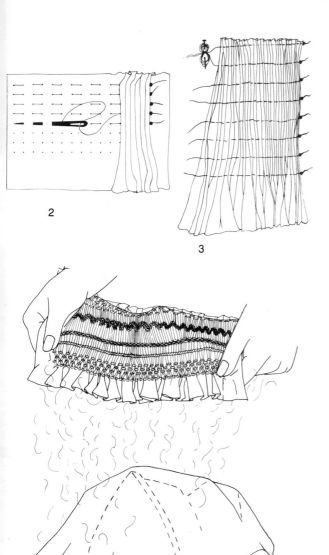

2

3

4

Now you are ready for the gathering. Thread a needle with enough strong cotton or quilting thread of a contrasting color to complete a row; joining is not possible. Begin at the right side, securing the thread firmly. Go in at one spot and out at the next so that when the fabric is drawn up, the gathering threads will run through the middle of the folds, holding the reeds firmly. On each succeeding row, repeat the previous one *exactly* so the vertical folds are formed evenly (Diagram 2).

When all of the gathering threads are in place, lay the fabric flat on the table and pull up on the threads in pairs until the folds lie side by side. Secure the gathering threads by twisting each pair around a pin placed at the left end of the reeds (Diagram 3).

When the gathering is complete, you are ready to start smocking. Secure the floss at the back of the first reed in each row. (Note that some stitches are worked across the row from left to right and others from right to left.) Take shallow stitches into the surface of each reed and follow the stitch arrangement here or create your own, using any of the stitches on page 148. Repeat a simple version of the pattern at the shoulders and wrists.

To finish and assemble the smock, first remove the gathering threads and steam the smocking. This is easily done by throwing a wet cloth over an iron and stretching the smocking in both directions so that the steam sets it to the desired width (Diagram 4).

Join the side seams two-thirds of the way up from the hem. Set in the shoulder straps. Join the sleeve seams from the wrist to within 7" of the top to allow the gussets to fit in. Set in sleeves and underarm gussets. Hem the shoulder strap backing in place.

To finish the front edges, you must add your button and buttonhole bands. Press under the seam allowance along the top, bottom, and one long edge of each band. Stitch the remaining long edge of each band to one of the edges at the front of the smock, right sides facing. Fold the band in half towards the back, forming self-facing, and slip stitch it into place. Work buttons (Diagram 5) and buttonholes. Set in the collar and hem.

5

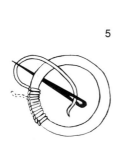

SMOCKING WITH A DIFFERENCE

The dress and top shown here both make use of smocking a little differently. The yoke of the wool jersey dress is smocked separately and added later, and the collar and cuffs of the organza jacket are done in the same way. Adding the smocking as a separate strip can make fitting easier, and it is certainly easier to handle a smaller piece of fabric while the stitching is being done.

On the yoke and the cuffs of the wool jersey dress, the "reeds" are suggested by close vertical rows of chain stitch (Diagram 1) which are caught together in spot honeycomb stitch (Diagram 2). This clever "pseudo-smocking" idea was designed by Tanya Josefowitz to eliminate bulk in the heavier weight material.

The collar and cuffs of the jacket were edged first with a spit and roll hem and cross-whipped in a contrasting color (Diagram 3). Then the smocking was joined to the top with a narrow seam. This can be easily done in a lightweight material such as organza or organdy and could be beautiful used with the handpainted silk technique shown on page 72. You can adapt commercial patterns for either of these ideas. Tanya's jersey dress was inspired by her nightdress!

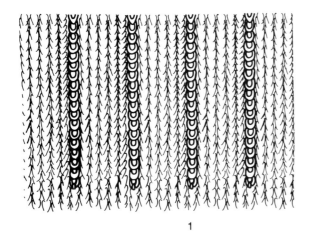

1

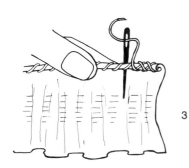

3

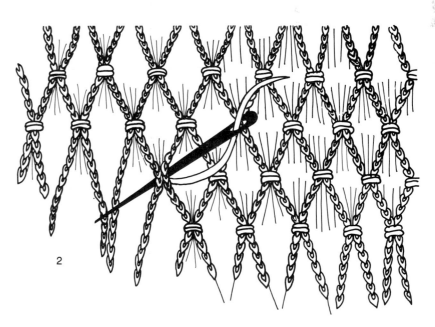

2

HANDBAGS

At one time handbags were worn in the form of pockets *under* a full skirt. Once out in the open, "pocketbooks" became decorative accessories made to match or to contrast with the wearer's dress.

The "sweet bags" given by Queen Elizabeth to her ladies of the court every New Year's Day are typical of these. The little drawstring bag opposite was inspired by one of the queen's bags, with the lace represented by cross-stitch and a wreath of wild flowers worked in fine scale in contrast to the bold white stitching. A scalloped border adds to the lacy effect and makes the mounting and finishing easy.

Often, the drawback to making your own handbags is the difficulty of mounting them. Most of the bags in this chapter are therefore of the drawstring or envelope varieties that can be easily mounted. None requires expensive professional help.

Another excellent technique for making bags, one which can be worked on plastic or regular canvas, is plaidpoint, a way of working a colorful tartan pattern in needlepoint. Its great advantage is that it is exactly alike on both sides, so the edges can be clean finished with broad bias wool tape. A knitting bag done in plaidpoint is pictured on page 97.

Crochet, fabric, needlepoint, gold thread embroidery, and ribbon weaving are all used in this chapter. All of the patterns and techniques shown here for bags would also be excellent for vests, tabard tops and, in many cases, for belts.

Left: Hand-tinted etching from Costumes Parisiens, *dated 1815. (The author's collection.)*

Opposite: The contrast of fine and bold cross-stitch on QUEEN ELIZABETH'S BAG gives the effect of lace, which is enhanced by the scalloped border.

Above: Burgundy wool and silver thread give the effect of weaving in a WOVEN NEEDLEPOINT BAG.

Opposite: WOVEN RIBBON HANDBAGS with a ruched effect, made with silk ribbons and gold cords.

Above: LANDSCAPE HANDBAG made with geometric stitches.

Right: WOVEN RIBBON HANDBAG with diagonal weaving.

Opposite: BUTTERFLY POUCH in satin and ORIENTAL BUT-TERFLY BAG in mock suede.

Opposite: Berlin Wool Work is the origin of the BERLIN BUTTERFLY BAG worked on canvas in cross-stitch. The design can also be adapted to counted cross-stitch.

Right: CROCHET BARREL BAG has a drawstring and is made with sleek rayon yarn and gold thread.

Below: FABRIC ENVELOPE BAG has three separate flaps that fold over to form a clutch. The center flap is done in crewel.

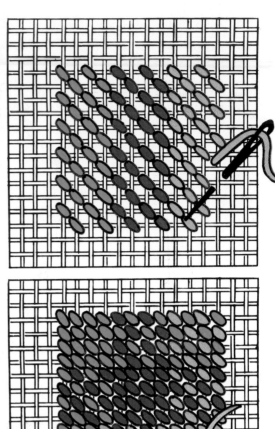

Above: To do the plaidpoint stitch, make a slanting stitch across one intersection of the canvas. Then, with the needle slanting as in the diagram, come up one thread below and repeat to form a vertical line, skipping every other stitch.

By slanting the needle as in the diagram, you will form an identical stitch on the reverse side. Be sure to work all the vertical lines first, using a thread long enough to complete each row. Start the next row one stitch down, creating a diagonal line as in the diagram.

When these vertical rows are completed, start on the horizontals. Now you fill in the gaps by working across horizontally, with exactly the same color sequence as in your vertical rows.

Left: RAINBOW TOTE BAG IN PLAIDPOINT.

RAINBOW TOTE BAG IN PLAIDPOINT

Plaidpoint is the fascinating technique of creating a Scottish plaid on needlepoint canvas. You work as though you are weaving, laying down all the threads in one direction and then stitching them through the opposite way. The result is colorful, durable, and reversible; it is ideal for handbags. Although you work this bag vertically and horizontally, once the circle is framed with a bias wool binding, you can turn it to make an attractive pattern of diamonds instead of squares.

Start by drawing a 14"-diameter circle on the canvas. With a pencil, draw intersecting vertical and horizontal lines along the straight of the canvas to establish the center. Begin by working the first vertical rows in red, right through the center, using three strands of yarn. Follow the color chart, working out from the center and making each color band eleven rows wide. When all of the vertical rows are worked, complete the horizontal rows, starting in the center and following the exact same color sequence.

Complete a second circle for the back of the bag. When both are stitched, you are ready to mount the bag. First, trim the canvas ½" away from the edge of the stitching. Clean finish edges with wool knit bias binding prefolded to 1".

The gusset and shoulder strap should be attached as one continuous strip of the same binding, unfolded to 2". Seam a piece of binding approximately 66" long. With right sides of the needlepoint facing, sew the strip to the inner edge of the binding, with the seam at the bottom of the bag. Leave approximately 18" for a top opening.

SHOPPING LIST
½ yard #10 canvas
Persian yarn in assorted colors
5 yards fold-over braid or
  wool knit bias binding

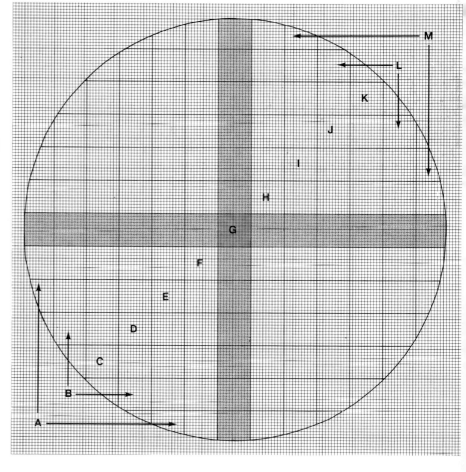

A—NAVY BLUE
B—DARK GREEN
C—BRIGHT GREEN
D—PLUM
E—BROWN
F—BRIGHT BLUE
G—RED
H—MOSS GREEN
I—DEEP ORANGE
J—YELLOW ORANGE
K—PALE BLUE
L—BEIGE
M—OFF-WHITE

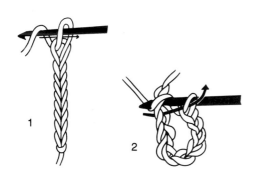

(Color photo, page 89.)

CROCHET BARREL BAG

This simple crochet bag is made of gold rayon yarn with real metal yarn to give it a sparkle. It would be equally effective worked with rayon ribbons in sunny colors as a daytime bag designed to go with a special outfit or with innovative fabrics such as string, waxed shoelace cording, or the ⅛"-wide simulated suede on spools now available for knitting and crochet.

Start by making the flat base of the bag. Make a chain (Diagram 1) of 15 stitches and join them with a slip stitch (Diagram 2) to form a ring. Row 1: Ch 1, turn. Sc (Diagram 3) into each ch, inc 5 st, spacing them evenly across the row. (This means you will work 2 single st every third ch to give you a total of 20 st.) To link circle, sl st into the first sc (Diagram 4) , ch 1 st, turn. Rows 2-13: Rep row 1. (To inc 5 st in each row, spacing them evenly, means row 2, inc every 4th st, row 3, inc in every 5th st, etc., for a total of 80 st to complete a base.) At the end of row 13, ch 3 in preparation for dc. Turn.

Row 14: Dc (Diagram 5) into each sc of previous row. Sl st into first dc, ch 4 (to prepare for tr). Turn. Row 15: Tr (Diagram 6) into each dc of previous row. Sl st into first tr, change to gold thread and ch 1. Sl st with gold yarn.

Row 16: Sc with gold yarn into tr from previous row. Sl st into first sc, ch 1 and turn. Row 17: Change to rayon yarn, ch 3 and rep row 16. Row 18: Dc rayon yarn into the gold sc from the previous row. Sl st into the first dc, change to gold yarn, ch 1 st with gold yarn.

Rows 19-36: Rep rows 16, 17, 18 six times. Bind off. On row 32, weave gold twisted cord through to form a drawstring.

SHOPPING LIST
2 balls rayon yarn (Melrose Cravenella) or Swade simulated suede
1 ball Camelot gold metallic yarn
#1 crochet hook

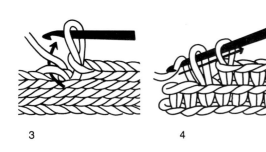

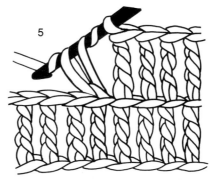

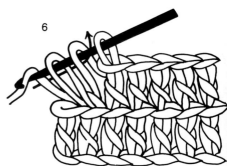

BERLIN BUTTERFLY BAG

A German printer at the turn of the century invented a system of colored graphs for cross-stitch designs on canvas. Known as Berlin Wool Work, it soon became so popular that special sheep were bred to provide the soft wool for the needlepoint.

You can work this bag on canvas exactly as it is shown or work in the technique which is as popular today as Berlin Work was in its time—counted cross-stitch.

If you work the design on #12 canvas with one strand of wool, the finished bag will measure 9½" × 13". If you work on 14-count even-weave fabric, use two to three strands of cotton floss. (Fiddler's cloth, a fabric with the look of an antique sampler, is especially attractive.)

Following the charts here, stitch the butterfly designs, placing them ten stitches apart as they are here or in any way suitable to your finished design. Note that the five stitches forming stars in the background are worked in a completely random manner, giving the pattern a lively effect.

You can line the bag with an attractive coordinating cotton print, edge with twisted cord (see page 116), and make a braided handle, using all of the colors from the butterflies.

(Color photo, page 88.)

SHOPPING LIST
½ yard #12 canvas or
   14-count even-weave fabric
Persian yarn or cotton floss
½ yard lining fabric

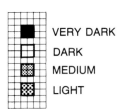

■ VERY DARK
□ DARK
▨ MEDIUM
▨ LIGHT

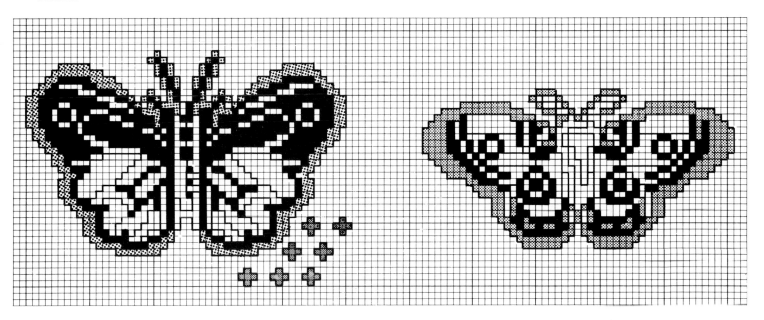

(Color photo, page 89.)

SHOPPING LIST
½ yard of three coordinating fabrics
  (one chintz, two solids)
crewel wools
fusible web interfacing
2 yards double-folded bias binding

First, find attractive fabrics for this clutch bag. Then, work the central flower in crewel with colors that blend with the fabrics you use.

Make three patterns on graph paper, enlarging the design in Diagram 1. Follow the full-size half pattern opposite to draw the curved lines, extending each piece on graph paper according to measurements given in Diagram 1. No seam allowances are necessary.

Outline pattern B on linen and trace the crewel flower design, positioning it as in the pattern. Mount the fabric in an embroidery frame and work the entire design in long and short stitch, with satin stitch in small areas.

For each of the pattern pieces, cut two identical pieces from fabric and one from fusible web, making each slightly larger than your paper pattern. To stiffen and line the bag, fuse these layers together with a hot iron, right sides of the fabric out. Finish the curved edges of each piece separately with bias binding, stack the pieces in the order given (Diagram 1), and join the three with bias binding around the three lower edges. Fold over the flaps as in the photograph, forming a bag with two separate pockets.

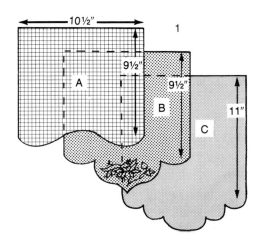

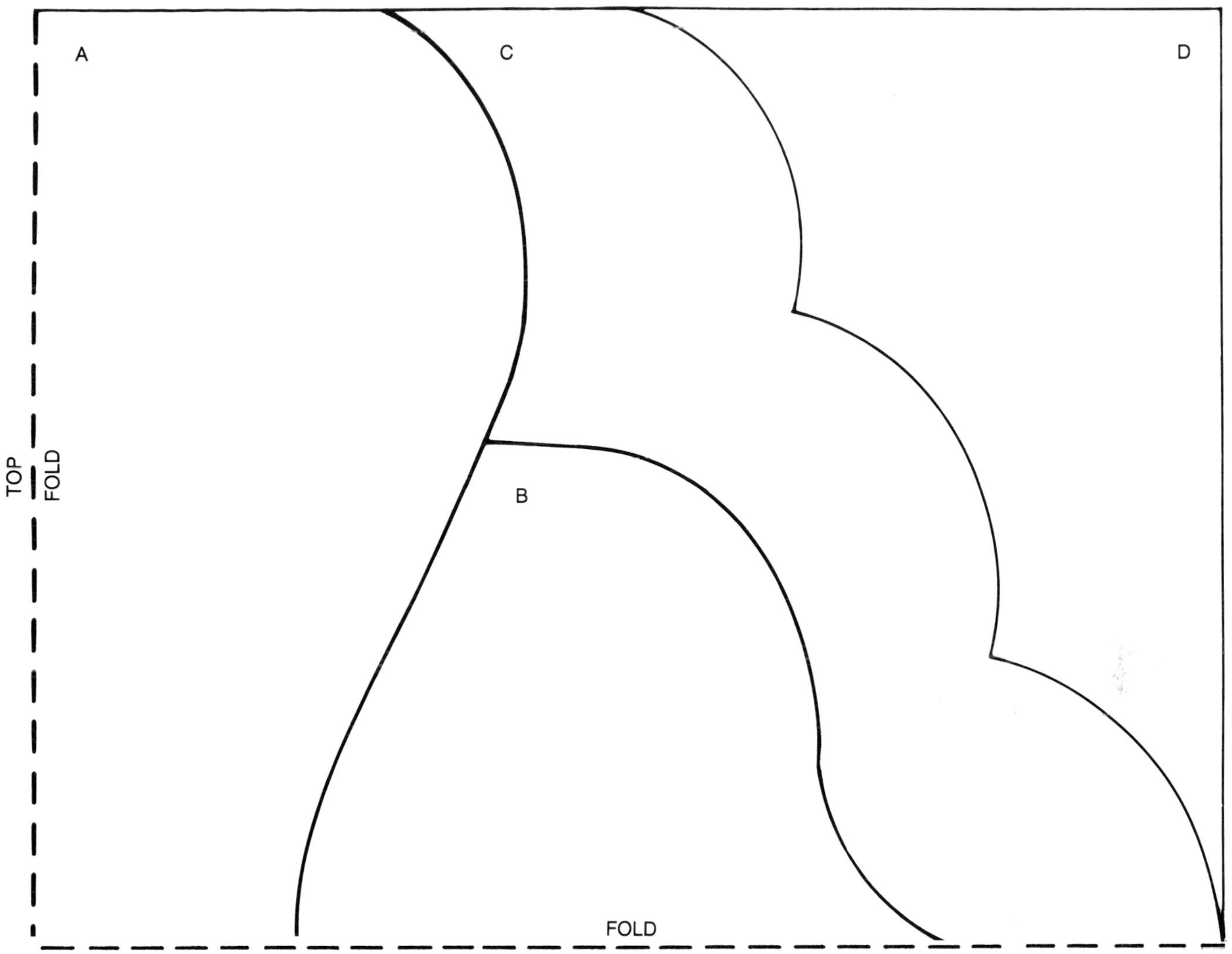

A

C

D

TOP

FOLD

B

FOLD

FULL-SIZE HALF PATTERN

FULL-SIZE PATTERN

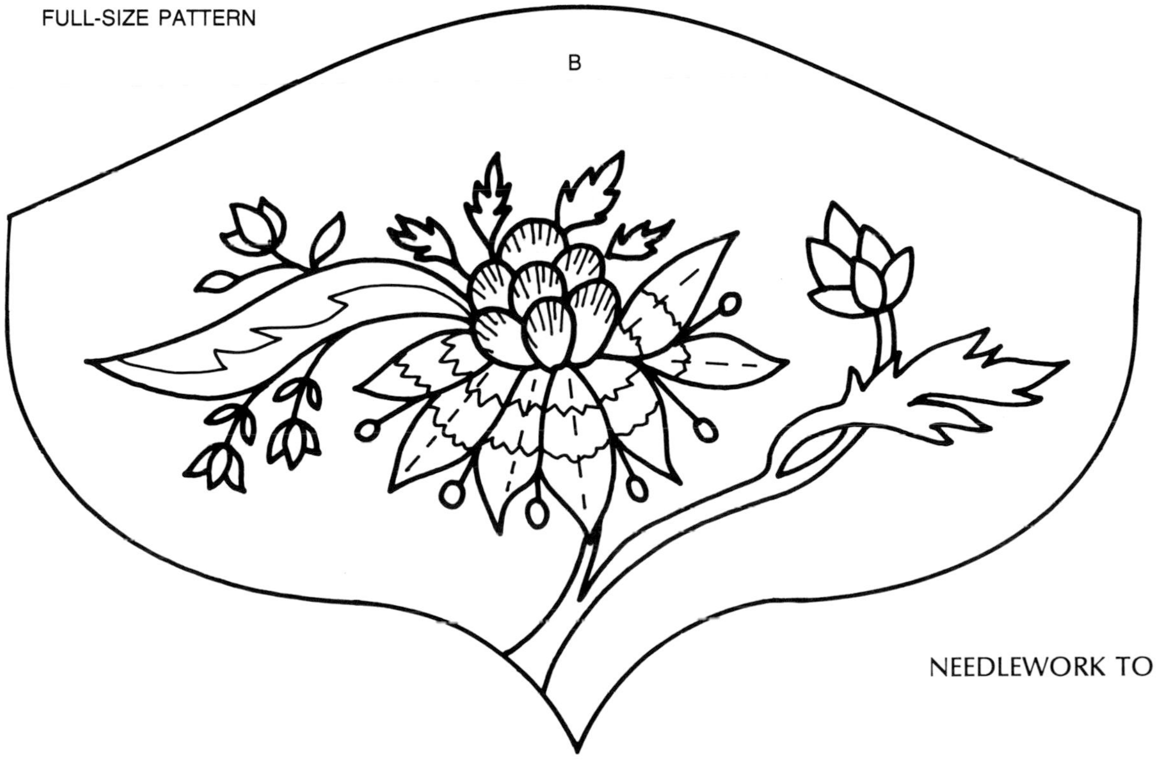

B

(Color photo, page 87.)

SHOPPING LIST
½ yard mock suede fabric
cotton or silk floss
Japanese gold thread
½ yard silk or cotton lining fabric
gold braid (optional)
wooden bead (optional)

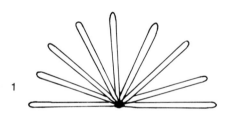
1

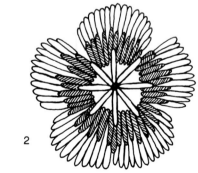
2

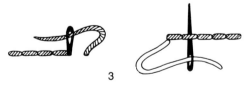
3

PEKINESE STITCH

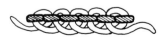

ORIENTAL BUTTERFLY BAG

This butterfly design was inspired by a delicate silk medallion on a robe from the Imperial Court in Peking. To the Chinese, butterflies are a symbol of everlasting life and happiness. The bag is worked on mock suede, which resembles velvet but will not fray; it is washable and crease-resistant.

Trace the full-size pattern and transfer it to fabric, positioning it as shown. With two strands of cotton floss, work the stitches in the following order.

Tree and all branches, slanting satin stitch; *leaves,* satin stitch; *pine needles,* straight stitches radiating from a single hole (Diagram 1); *blossoms,* long and short stitches, with centers straight stitches radiating from a single hole (Diagram 2); *butterfly wings and body,* satin stitch for small areas and long and short for wider spaces; *antennae,* chain with six strands of floss whipped with one strand of gold thread; *border,* Pekinese stitch with six strands of floss and one strand of gold thread (Diagram 3).

Using the pattern, trim the finished embroidery and the back of bag, leaving ½" seam allowances. Seam back and front together, right sides facing, leaving the top open.

Cut two pieces for the lining from the same pattern and seam them together, rights sides facing, leaving the top open. Turn inside out and slip the bag *into* the lining. (Reverse sides will be facing.)

To finish the top and make a channel for the drawstring, fold the top of the bag down 2" over the lining. Machine stitch two parallel lines ⅜" apart just above the lower edge.

Turn the bag right side out. Cut a small slit on each side, between the machine stitched lines, to receive drawstring.

Make two lengths of twisted cord 40" long from two full strands of 80"-long cotton floss (page 116). With a blunt needle, thread the first cord through the machine stitched channel, starting at one side, threading all the way around, and returning to the same side. Overlap cord ends, sew them firmly together, and ease the join into the channel so it doesn't show. Repeat with the second cord, threading from the opposite side.

Couch metal thread or gold braid around the top edge of the bag. If desired, make a tassel from floss and thread its end through a floss-wrapped wooden bead. Sew to the bottom of the bag.

FULL-SIZE PATTERN

FOLD LINE

- -

- -

CHANNEL FOR CORDING

- -

97

(Color photo, page 87.)

SHOPPING LIST
½ yard satin
cotton floss, including
 one color of ombré
Japanese gold thread
lameflex gold thread
1 yard grosgrain fabric
¾ yard Pellon® interfacing
heavy cord

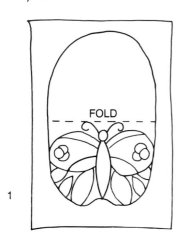

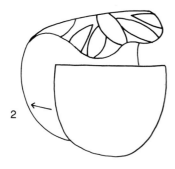

BUTTERFLY POUCH

Both this bag and the Oriental Butterfly on the previous page are worked in the Chinese tradition, with geometric patterns formed within the naturalistic shapes. This gives great scope for the texture of the stitches and means that the shades can easily be changed to coordinate with any color scheme. The bag would look magnificent in white, cream, off-white and silver, for instance, mixing wool, floss, and metal thread on white fabric.

Make a paper pattern of the bag by folding a 12″ × 16″ piece of tracing paper in quarters to establish its center. Unfold the paper and trace the outline and design on the unshaded area of the pattern under the fold. Turn the paper upside down and trace the outline of the whole pattern, including the shaded area, on the other side of the fold, taking care to match up side lines.

Mount the satin in an embroidery frame and transfer the design and the bag outline to it. Stitch the design in alphabetical order, following the chart. Use three strands of cotton floss unless otherwise noted.

A. *Leaves,* close herringbone in ombré floss; *stems,* Pekinese stitch (backstitch with six threads of floss and weave one strand of Japanese gold). B. *Centers,* couching in a circle with Japanese gold; *outlines,* three rows of stem stitch with floss. C. As A, but stems are close herringbone changing to stem stitch. D. Padded satin stitch. E. Fill ground rows of split stitch following broken lines on chart. F. Close herringbone in ombré floss. G. Leave fabric open. H. Rope stitch outlined with couched Japanese gold. J. Laid work, vertically with ombré floss. Crisscross lines in lameflex gold.

When embroidery is finished, cut out the bag, leaving ¼″ all around for seam allowances. Cut interfacing and grosgrain lining the same size. Stack the lining and embroidered fabric right sides together with the interfacing on top. Stitch, leaving an opening on one side for turning. Turn right side out and blind stitch the opening, resulting in the outside back and the front flap of the pouch (Diagram 1).

To form the front pocket, make a paper pattern using the curved shape of the back as your guide. This front pocket should be 6″ deep with ¼″ seam allowances all around. Cut out two pieces of grosgrain and one piece of interfacing from the new pattern and clean finish exactly as you did the body of the bag. Blind stitch the back and front of the bag together (Diagram 2) to form the pocket (Diagram 3).

Edge the bag and make shoulder straps with heavy cord.

FOLD LINE

(Color photo, page 86.)

(Color photo, page 85.)

WOVEN RIBBON HANDBAGS

With colorful ribbons, you can weave beautiful patterns and then fuse them to interfacing to make handbags, belts, vests, jackets, or slippers and clogs. You can make either diagonal or straight-woven handbags by following these instructions.

Cut an 8″ × 17½″ piece of fusible interfacing and place it on your ironing board, fusible side up. Cut enough strips of ribbon to cover the interfacing and place them diagonally over it, lined up next to each other. Pin the ends of each ribbon to the ironing board.

Cut another set of ribbons and weave them diagonally over and under the first set (Diagram 1). Anchor with pins at both ends. When all ribbons have been woven, fuse them in place, using a press cloth and steam.

If you prefer the ruched effect shown in the lower photograph, create a vertical warp by winding cord up and down over pins (Diagram 2). Then weave in the ribbons, packing them together as you go with a knitting needle.

To mount the bag, lay lining fabric on top, right sides facing. Stitch around the edges, leaving one side open. Turn right sides out and blind stitch the opening closed. Fold the bag into an envelope shape and sew fasteners in place. Blind stitch the sides together and attach a chain and loose ribbons to the sides of the bag.

SHOPPING LIST
fusible interfacing (white for a light
 color scheme, black for a dark)
Offray® decorative ribbons
 in varying lengths
gold metal cord or piping
lining fabric
snap closing
gold chain

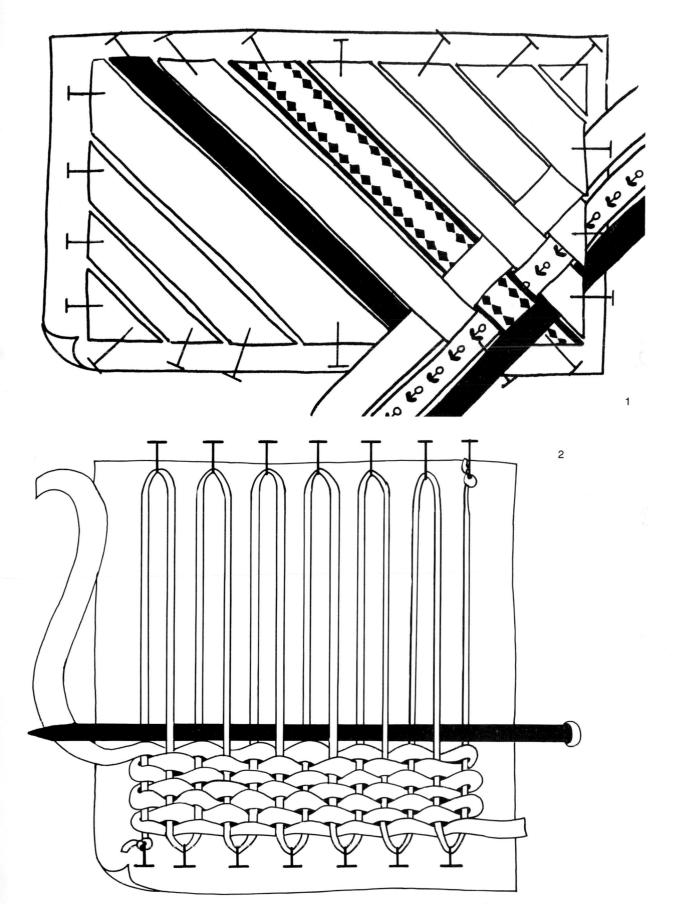

1

2

(Color photo, page 84.)

WOVEN NEEDLEPOINT BAG

This very tailored bag gives a *trompe l'oeil* effect of weaving. In the photo, the finished bag is shown with alternating lines of stitching and open canvas. The bag in work on the frame is shown with silver thread alternated with burgundy wool.

Mark the desired area for the bag on canvas. Using two strands of burgundy yarn and one strand of silver, stitch horizontally as follows: Rows 1 and 2, burgundy; row 3, silver; row 4, burgundy; row 5, silver; rows 6 and 7, burgundy; row 8, four stitches of silver, four of burgundy, four of silver, etc.

Repeat this pattern from the first row until the area is covered. For mounting, see instructions for mounting an envelope bag, page 150.

SHOPPING LIST
½ yard #14 interlock canvas
burgundy Persian yarn
Camelot silver thread
cardboard or illustration board
rayon or moiré lining fabric
gold chain

LANDSCAPE HANDBAG

This envelope bag is made on needlepoint canvas in geometric stitches. First, the canvas is colored. Then the stitches are worked, leaving threads between to allow the mesh to show through for an attractive geometric effect.

Transfer the design from the full-size outline with black permanent marker. Cover the canvas design, including an area three inches all around the design, with gray permanent marker. Allow to dry.

Using four strands of cotton floss, work the stitches, following the diagrams. Now couch Supra Swade around the edges with one thread of matching cotton floss, bricking the stitches in each succeeding row. Work two rows around the design and ten rows across the top, folding the strips at corners to make neat turns.

For mounting instructions for this bag, see page 150.

SHOPPING LIST
½ yard #14 canvas
black and gray permanent markers
cotton floss
Supra Swade (see Suppliers)
fabric for lining
Sobo glue
suede cloth

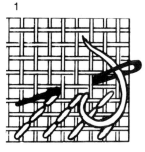

1

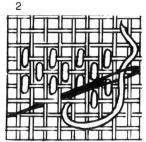

2

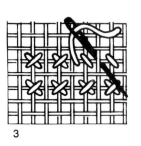

3

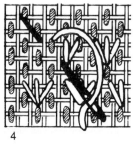

4

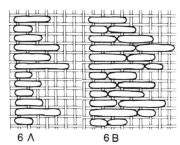

5

6 A   6 B

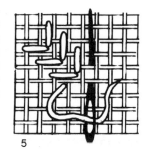

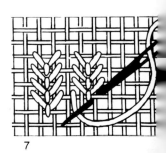

7

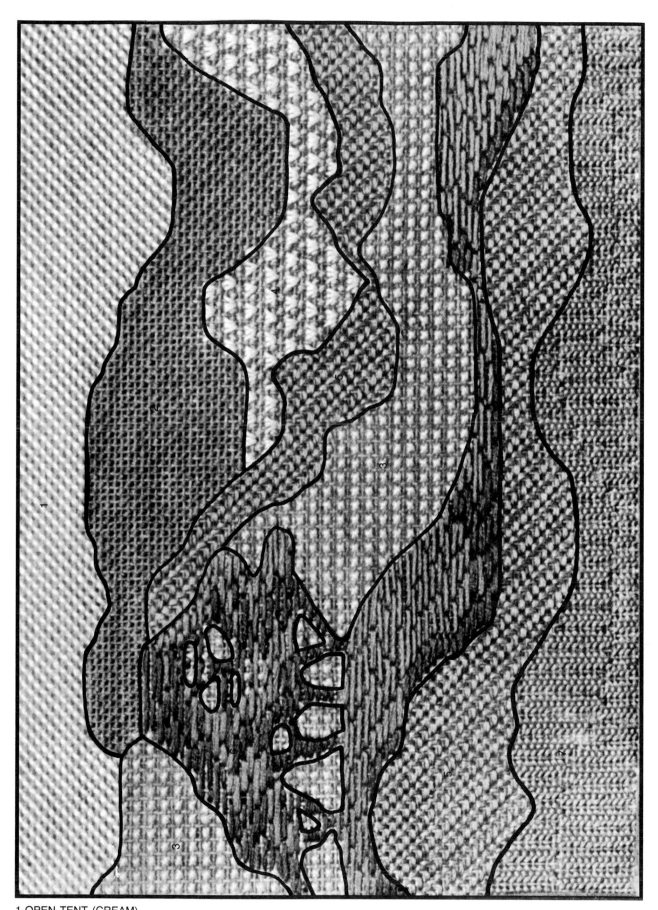

1-OPEN TENT (CREAM)
2-BRICK (DEEP BLUE)
3-CROSS (GRAY)
4-CROWSFEET ON SPACED BRICK (LIGHT BLUE WITH CREAM)
5-REVERSE TENT (MAUVE)
6A, B-LONG AND SHORT (LIGHT BLUE, DEEP OLIVE)
7-FISHBONE (TAN)

(Color photo, page 83.)

SHOPPING LIST
½ yard 14-count Aida cloth
  or Fiddler's cloth
cotton floss
10 (½"-diameter) white plastic
  curtain rings
½ yard red moiré fabric for lining

QUEEN ELIZABETH'S BAG

This drawstring bag with cross-stitched lace and scalloped border is just like one of the little "Sweet Bags" given by Queen Elizabeth to her ladies in waiting every New Year's Day. They contained money and were very often aromatic with lavender, rose petals or cloves.

To make the bag, begin by mounting fabric on stretcher strips or in an embroidery hoop. Using contrasting thread, baste intersecting vertical and horizontal lines to establish the center point marked on the chart. Note that the medallion falls below center because the bag is oblong.

Using six strands of white cotton floss and working over two threads of the mesh, work the center lace pattern, counting from the graph. Next, with two strands of floss, work the floral wreath over one thread of the mesh, using the colors shown in the photograph on page 83 or your own color scheme.

Work the cross-stitch lace design around the wreath and the outer edge. Cross-stitch the same pattern for the back of the bag, if desired.

Pin and baste the front and back panels, wrong sides together, leaving the top and 3" down each side open. Cover the curtain rings by buttonholing with four strands of white floss. Stitch five rings on each side of the bag, spacing them evenly just below the upper lace border.

To make the scalloped border, fold a piece of 12" × 16" tracing paper in quarters. Place this over the quarter scallop border here, with folded paper edges towards the top and right side. Trace the scallops 1" in from the edge of the paper. Cut out the scallops, discard the center, and open up the paper to form a frame. Position this over your finished design, making certain the border motif fits in the center of each scallop. Trace.

Using two strands of white floss, buttonhole the edges of the front and back pieces of fabric together, loops to the outside. Make the lining, slip it to the inside, and buttonhole it to the bag along the upper edges and the three open scallops on each side.

Make two one-yard twisted cords from floss (page 116). Thread one length of cord through the curtain rings, knotting its ends together on one side. Thread the other length of cord the opposite way to form the drawstring.

CHART FOR CROSS-STITCH

FULL-SIZE SCALLOP PATTERN (¼ OF BAG)

BELTS & COLLARS

The Elizabethans knew how flattering a lace ruff framing the face could be. Collars and belts have once more come into their own. Instead of being mere accessories, they can be the focal point of your whole costume.

Collars can be made with cutwork or appliqué, or they can be splendid with couched gold thread like the Lotus Petal Collar on page 128, which was inspired by a Chinese emperor's robes.

The word lace is almost synonymous with the word collar. Surprising as it seems, the sewing machine was originally invented to duplicate expensive handmade laces; only later was it discovered that it could also be used for sewing seams! In a magnificent handkerchief given to Queen Victoria, which included a combination of handmade and machine-made lace, it was impossible to see where one lace ended and the other began. You can buy a ready-made machine lace collar or make one from antique lace, and add your own touches in the form of beading. The collar on page 110 shows this, with tiny seed pearl beads, giving the effect of dewdrops, accenting the design.

Belts can be braided, twisted from ropes, jewelled, or couched in gold like those opposite, or they can be made from fat tubes of fabric like the one shown on page 114. You can also make belts with the lanyard weaving technique shown on page 24, or with woven ribbons like the handbag on page 100. Another idea is to use the butterfly chart on page 93 to make an unusual needlepoint belt, either with butterflies repeated all around or with a single butterfly worked and cut out to form the clasp.

The jewelled belt opposite is owned and modelled by my friend Frank Butler. It was given to him by the Maharaja of Jaipur and was done in the Indian technique of setting stones in with raised gold threads.

Left: Portrait dated 1587. (Royal Academy of Arts, London.)

Opposite: BELT BUCKLES OR NUÉ (top) are gold threads couched on needlepoint canvas; JEWELLED BELT (center) with cabuchon stones; WRAPPED JUTE BRAIDS and softly wrapped ribbons (bottom).

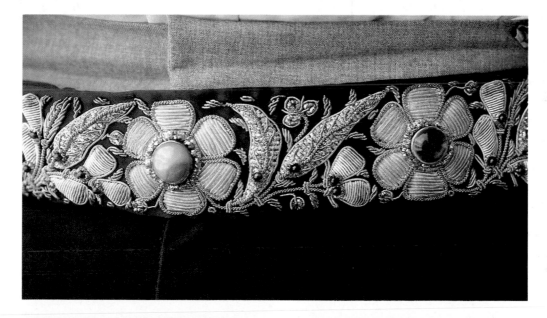

RAISED FLOWER PETAL COLLAR

Opposite: Tubes of fabric can be braided or can become POP-IN FLOWER BELTS.

Opposite: Pearl beads stitched to lace give the effect of dewdrops on a spider's web in this BEADED LACE COLLAR.

Below: Sheer fabric and delicate stit... make this ORGANZA CUTWORK COLLAR.

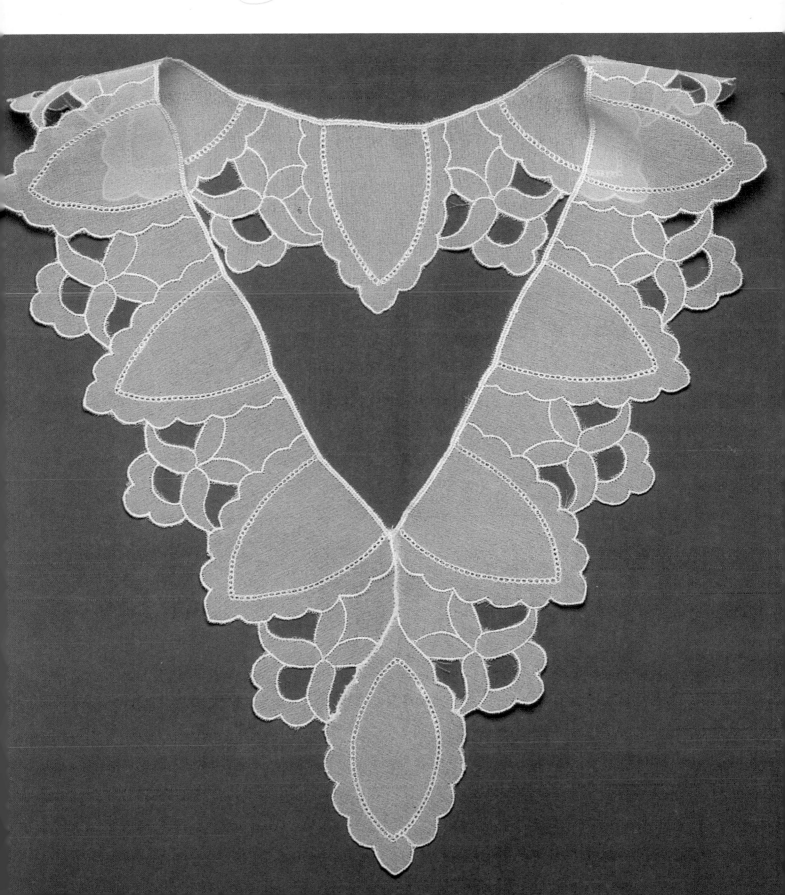

Opposite: Learn simple techniques to make your own DESIGNER BELTS.

Below: Couched gold and Chinese Openwork versions of the LOTUS PETAL COLLAR.

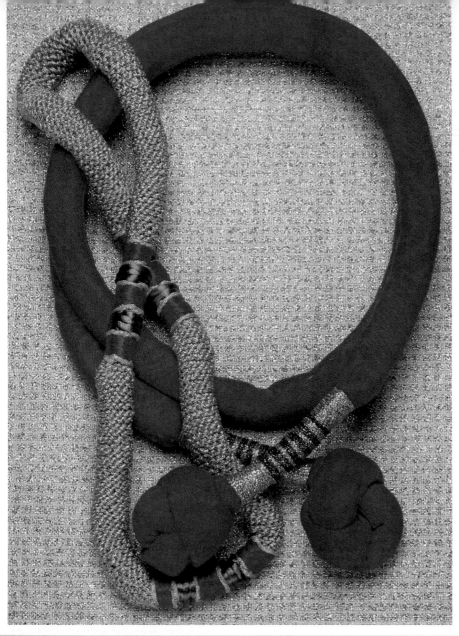

Left: Knitted and stuffed TUBE BELT OR NECKLACE.

Below: CORDS, TWISTS & BRAIDS can be made from any material.

TUBE BELT OR NECKLACE

The knitted tube opposite may be used as a belt, a bracelet, or a necklace. It could also be knitted wider and left unstuffed to wear as a flat, silky belt with a soft buckle.

The technique for knitting a tube is simple. Cast on six stitches and, in the first row, increase one in every stitch to make twelve stitches. In every row after that, purl the first stitch, slip the second, purl the third, and so on. Continue alternating purl and slip stitches until the end of the row. Always work with an even number of stitches so that the last stitch of each row is a slip stitch and the first stitch of each row is a purl stitch. Continue until the desired length is reached.

To cast off, pick up every other stitch on one side of the needle with a safety pin or holding pin. With the other needle, pick up the remaining stitches from the other side of the needle and cast them off. Put the stitches from the safety pin onto the needle and cast off. This results in an open tube.

Attach a strong thread to a length of drapery weights. (These continuous strips of fabric-covered weights are sold in notions stores.) Thread a blunt needle and pull the weights through the tube. To make a necklace, wrap sections of the tube about 5½" apart with gold metallic or rattail cord, using the invisible wrapping technique below. Join the two ends by overlapping them, tacking them in place, and invisibly wrapping the join with the same cord. To make a belt, make fat knots just below the wrappings at both ends of the tube.

SHOPPING LIST
#4 knitting needles
Melrose Cravenella Bronze yarn
drapery weights (by the yard)
heavy-weight yarn
gold metallic or rattail cord

THE INVISIBLE WRAPPING TECHNIQUE

Many of the projects in this book call for wrapping. By using this method, you can easily end the wrapping threads securely and invisibly.

Form a loop a bit longer than the wrapping will be and hold it in position *under* your wrapping cord (Diagram 1). When you have reached the end of your wrapping, thread the end of your cord through the loop (Diagram 2). Using the tail at the start of the wrapping, pull the loop and the end under the wrapping (Diagram 3). Pull tightly to tie a firm knot under the wrapping and trim ends.

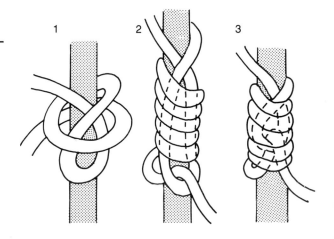

(Color photo, page 114.)

CORDS, TWISTS, AND BRAIDS

Cords, twists, and braids have come into their own once more. They are available ready-made, or you can make your own to use for belts, jewelry, or handbags.

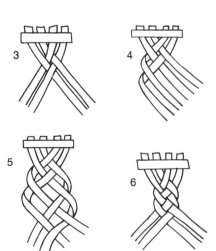

TWISTED CORD

To make a cord, knot two lengths of virtually any kind of thread together at each end. Secure one end to any firm object. Insert a pencil at the other end and turn it to twist the threads until you have a single, tightly twisted length of thread (Diagram 1). Then fold the length in half and allow the thread to twist back on itself into a nice, thick cord. (Diagram 2). Stroke it smooth and knot the open end.

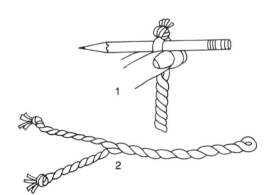

BRAIDING WITH FOUR

Tape two pairs of ribbons to a firm object, angling the pairs towards each other (Diagram 3). Now, weave the right-hand ribbons through the left-hand pair as in the diagram. Next, fold the left-hand ribbons *towards you,* parallel with the right-hand ribbons (Diagram 4). Then fold the right ribbons *away from you* and weave them under, over, and under the left-hand pair (Diagram 5). Repeat, continuing to fold the left-hand ribbons parallel with those on the right and always weaving with the right-hand pair (Diagram 6).

ROLLING BO'SUN

This attractive cord develops as a spiral. Starting with four strands, knot two opposite strands together (Diagram 7). Then knot the other two over the first knot, allowing the cord to twist around as you knot (Diagram 8). Using two colors will help you to keep the pairs separate as you continue to knot opposites together (Diagram 9).

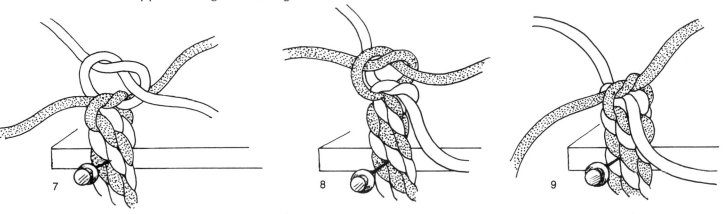

WRAPPED JUTE BRAIDS

Braid three groups of jute 42″ long. Wrap the center 14″ with wide ribbon, using masking tape to hold the ends in position as you work (Diagram 10). Next, wrap two rows of rattail cord in different colors, followed by one row of narrow ribbon; follow with a row of gold braid (Diagram 11).

Using the invisible wrapping technique (page 115), cover the ends of the previous wrappings with gold thread. To finish each end, fold over a loop and invisibly wrap it in place with gold (Diagram 12).

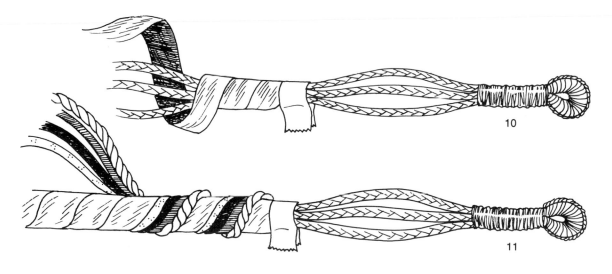

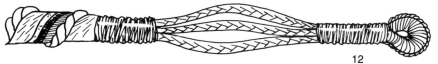

(Color photo, page 109.)

POP-IN FLOWER BELTS

SHOPPING LIST
cotton fabric in solids,
  prints, or calicoes
string
heavy acrylic or rug yarn
cotton balls (optional)

Blossoms of calico prints and polka dots can be used at the ends of fabric braids. Smaller flowers can be used to appliqué on a collar or sweater.

Cut bias strips 36" to 48" in length; for a belt with several flowers, vary the length of each strip so flowers will fall at different levels. Fold the fabric lengthwise so that right sides are facing and enclose a piece of string that is longer than the bias strip in the fold. Machine stitch a line ¼" in from the fold, securing one end of the string in the process. Pull on the string to turn the strip right side out; cut the string off and discard it.

To stuff, double several strands of yarn in a blunt, large needle and pull them through.

To make each flower petal, cut a circle of fabric, fold it in half (Diagram 1), double it over, and run a gathering thread through all four layers along the curved edge (Diagram 2). You can then connect five more petals with the same gathering thread, draw it up into a circle, and connect the ends to make a ring of petals (Diagram 4).

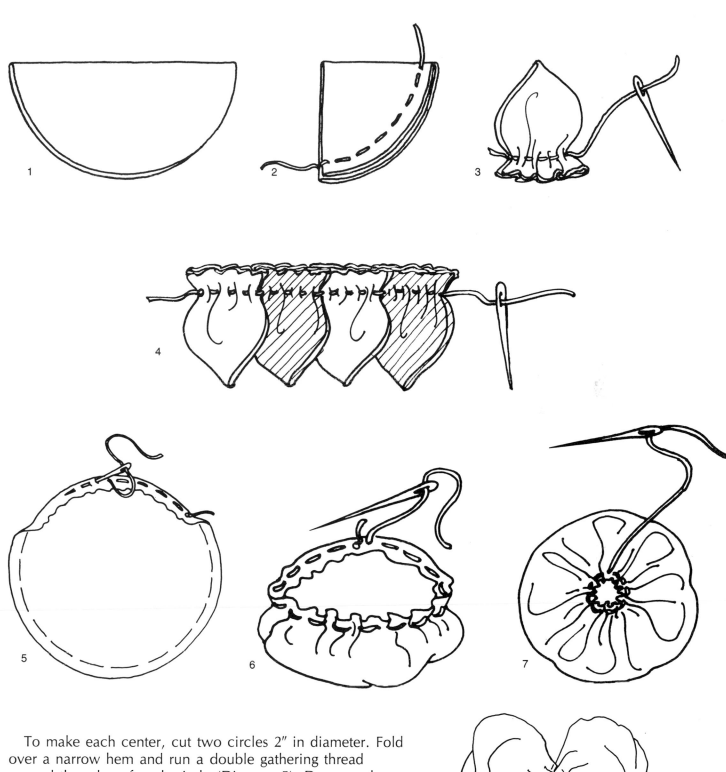

To make each center, cut two circles 2″ in diameter. Fold over a narrow hem and run a double gathering thread around the edge of each circle (Diagram 5). Draw up the gathering thread (Diagrams 6 and 7). Sew two circles together (Diagram 8) and pop them into your ring of petals. Secure each with a few invisible stitches before sewing to the ends of the belt. (For a raised effect, you can stuff each circle with a cotton ball before joining pairs.)

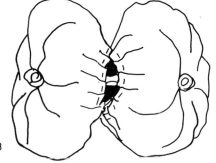

(Color photo, page 108.)

SHOPPING LIST
½ yard linen
cotton floss
½ yard silk or chintz
Versatex fabric paint (optional)
interfacing
thin batiste or muslin for backing

RAISED FLOWER PETAL COLLAR

The flowers on this collar look like a drift of cherry blossoms that has fallen on the grass in spring. You can paint your own flowers on silk fabric or cut out the flowers from a printed chintz fabric, attaching them to the background only at their centers to give them a three-dimensional effect.

Fold a piece of tracing paper in half and, using the half outline given, draw a full collar pattern. Trace the pattern onto the linen, marking the position of each flower as shown. Mount the fabric in an embroidery frame and work a double row of stem stitch ⅛" from the border.

To make silk flowers as shown in the photograph, outline the flowers from the patterns on silk and paint with fabric paint (see page 44). When dry, outline each flower by hand with the trailing stitch shown here, with whipped chain stitch, or by machine, using a close, narrow zigzag stitch. Trailing is done by taking fine whipping stitches closely over a bundle of three or more loose threads, forming the effect of a smooth, raised cord. Come up at A, go over the bundle of threads, and go down at B, almost in the same hole as A (Diagram 1). Repeat, placing stitches closely side by side. As you take each stitch, pull the bundle of couching threads firmly in the direction you are working (Diagram 2). This helps make the line smooth and firm.

Cut out each flower close to the stitching and position, pin, and baste all of them on the collar. Secure the center of each flower to the collar with five small clusters of yellow satin stitch radiating from the center and one circle of purple satin stitch at the center. Connect the flowers visually with stems done in a double row of stem stitch.

Lay the finished collar, right side up, on top of a piece of interfacing. Lay the sheer backing fabric on top of the collar. To be sure the collar will set well, check to be sure that the grain of the fabrics for the collar and the lining are parallel and aligned. Baste and machine stitch the three fabrics together, leaving an opening at the center of the back for turning. Trim and notch seam allowances and press seams open to make smooth curves. Turn the collar right side out and blind stitch the opening closed. The collar can be secured with a small button or with twisted cords.

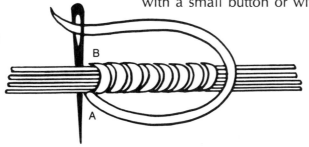

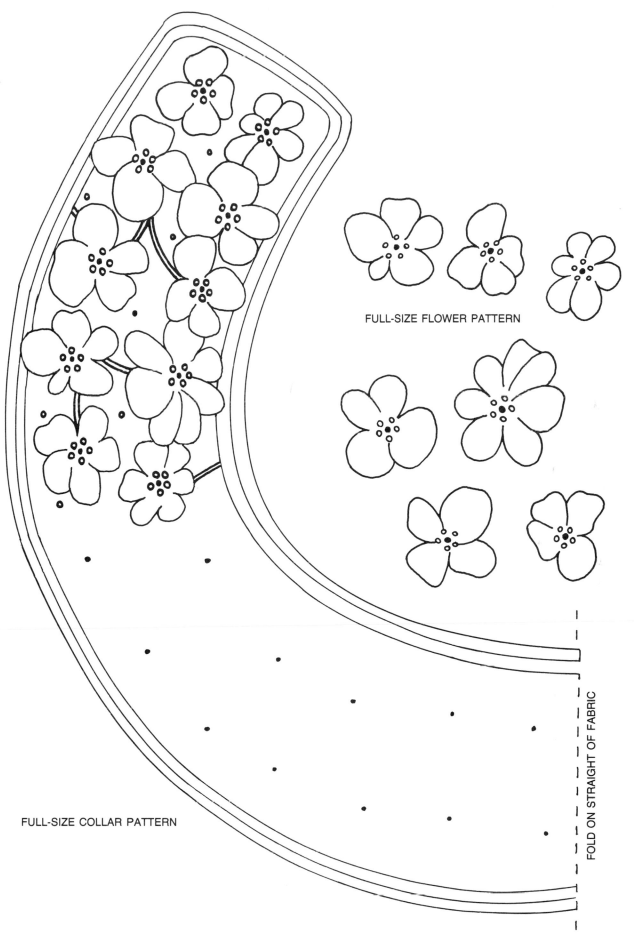

FULL-SIZE FLOWER PATTERN

FULL-SIZE COLLAR PATTERN

FOLD ON STRAIGHT OF FABRIC

121

(Color photo, page 110.)

BEADED LACE COLLAR

SHOPPING LIST
vinyl shelf paper
ready-made lace collar or
   ½ yard tulle and
   scraps of lace
beading needles
nylon beading thread
pearl beads

Beads can add just the right amount of weight and substance to a ready-made lace collar. Pearl beads that closely match the color of the background highlight the lace, adding a glint of light here and there.

Cut a rectangle of vinyl shelf paper slightly larger than the collar and baste the collar to it. (Giving the flimsy lace a firm backing makes beading easier—the needle glances off the vinyl surface without catching the backing.)

To start, thread your needle with *both* ends of a doubled thread. Take a small stitch into the fabric and, when coming up, thread the needle through the loop at the end of the doubled thread (Diagram 1). Transfer the beads onto the needle from their original string (Diagram 2). Sew them down in rows, or individually, ending off securely with backstitches.

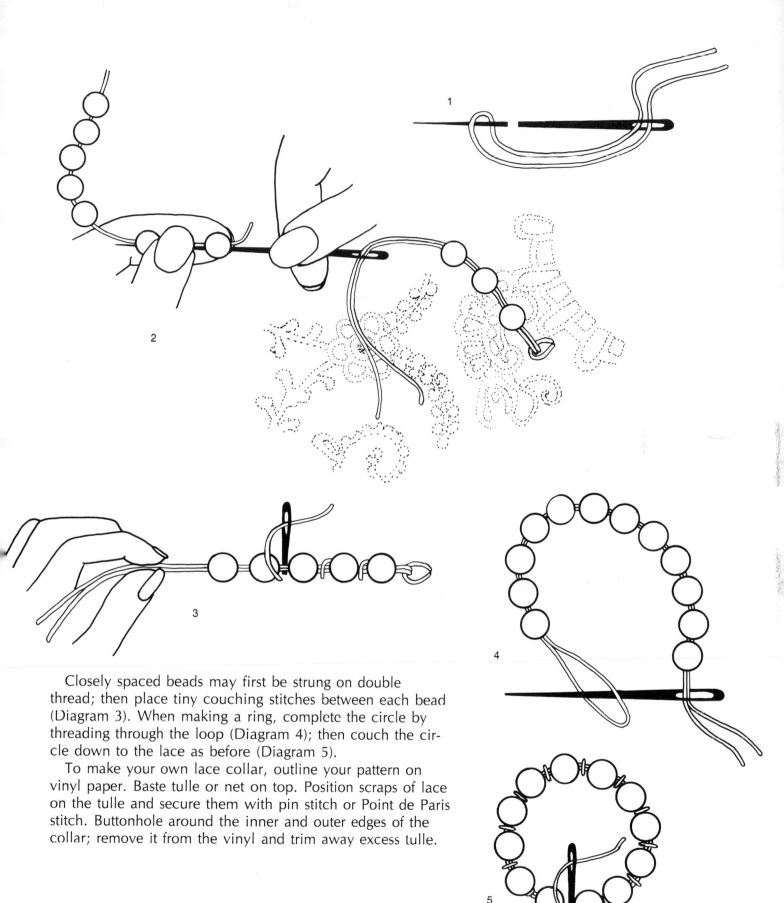

Closely spaced beads may first be strung on double thread; then place tiny couching stitches between each bead (Diagram 3). When making a ring, complete the circle by threading through the loop (Diagram 4); then couch the circle down to the lace as before (Diagram 5).

To make your own lace collar, outline your pattern on vinyl paper. Baste tulle or net on top. Position scraps of lace on the tulle and secure them with pin stitch or Point de Paris stitch. Buttonhole around the inner and outer edges of the collar; remove it from the vinyl and trim away excess tulle.

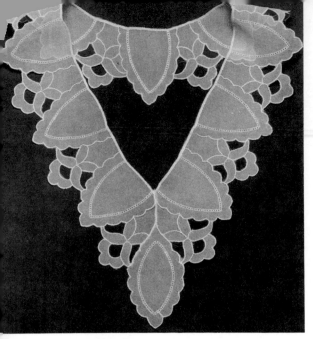

(Color photo, page 111.)

SHOPPING LIST
½ yard fabric (organza, organdy,
  fine batiste, or lawn)
cotton floss
bias binding
fusible web (optional)

POINT TURC (PUNCH) STITCH

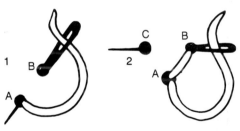

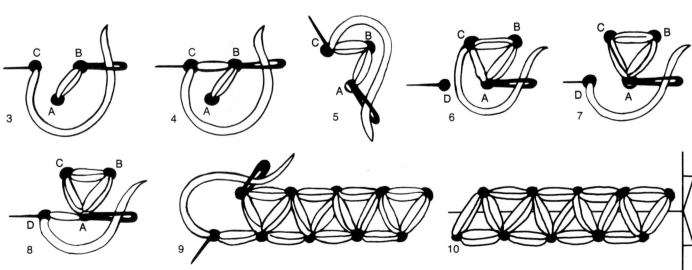

ORGANZA CUTWORK COLLAR

The attractive cutwork design of this collar could be used in different ways. To make a V neck as shown, trace the full-size patterns opposite on paper. Unfold the paper, join back to front (A to A) and fit the pattern over your V-neck sweater or blouse. If the V is deeper or shorter than the pattern, simply make the collar with an opening at the center back and adjust the pattern accordingly.

Alternatively, make a Peter Pan collar like the one on page 108. Trace three full backs. Then cut out the center leaf and the two flowers on either side of it to make an opening at the center front.

With a Trace Erace™ pen or hard pencil, transfer the two pattern pieces to fabric. With one single strand of cotton floss, outline all edges with buttonhole stitch, loops to outside. Using a large blunt needle, work the inner openwork line with Point de Paris or Point Turc stitch. Either of these two stitches may be used to join the back section to the front with a decorative seam.

When complete, carefully trim the fabric close to the stitching. Plunge sharp-pointed scissors into the center of each area to be cut away and snip out to the corners. Finish the inner edge of the collar with narrow bias binding and lightly hem the collar to your blouse. (This edging allows you to easily remove the collar for separate cleaning.)

If you find working on sheer fabric with tiny buttonhole stitches too delicate, an easy way to achieve a similar effect is to fuse two layers of organza together with the lightest weight fusible web and to work all the outlines with chain stitch by hand or machine. You will then find the stiff fabric can easily be cut away.

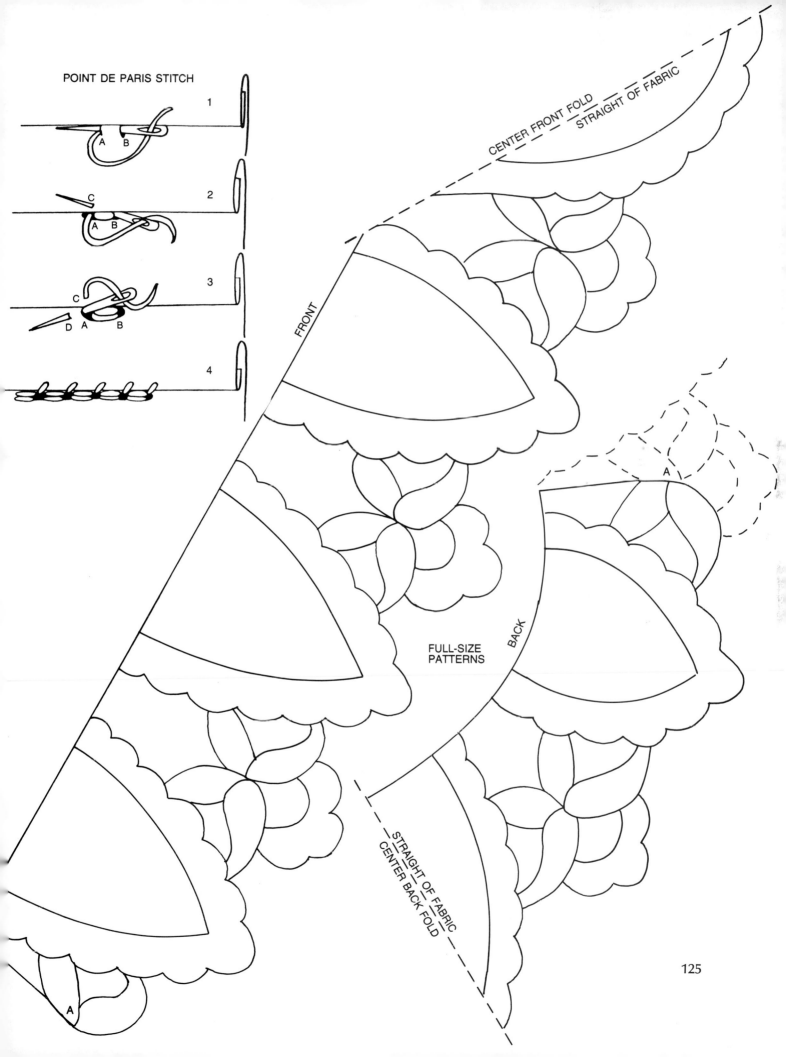

POINT DE PARIS STITCH

1

2

3

4

CENTER FRONT FOLD
STRAIGHT OF FABRIC

FRONT

FULL-SIZE
PATTERNS

BACK

A

STRAIGHT OF FABRIC
CENTER BACK FOLD

A

125

(Color photo, page 107.)

SHOPPING LIST
30-mesh gauze, fine interlock canvas,
  or linen
Japanese gold thread
silk thread
cotton floss
needles (#8 or #9 crewel for gauze
  or linen; #20 tapestry for canvas)
cardboard
all-purpose glue
backing fabric

BELT BUCKLES OR NUÉ

The technique of couching rows of metal thread to completely cover the background is called *Or Nué* or Italian Shading. You build up the design row by row, closely covering the gold with colored silk floss to give the effect of enamel work or metallic brocade. These stunning belt buckles can also be made as pins or pendants.

Transfer one of the full-size patterns here to fabric, lining up the intersecting vertical and horizontal lines on your design with the weave of the fabric. (For beginners, the simpler design is the morning glory, which does not have shading.)

Start at the top, couching in brick stitch and working in horizontal rows. Work over two threads of Japanese gold thread with one thread in any color that closely matches your gold. At the end of each row, turn the corner (Diagrams 1 and 2) and work in the opposite direction. From the second row onward, come up with your couching thread below the gold and go in above it, sharing the holes from the previous row. This technique keeps the rows of gold close together, with no fabric showing in between.

Thread one needle with each of the colors to be used in the design. Work across the row, introducing the colors one by one as the design calls for them. Completely cover the gold with the colored thread where necessary, but leave it uncovered in the other areas. Continue to couch the background in brick stitch with matching thread. (Diagram 3.)

When the stitching is finished, mount the belt buckle, using the same method as in the medallion on page 32. Attach the buckle to decorative wide elastic or other banding, using hooks and eyes for fastening.

FULL-SIZE PATTERN

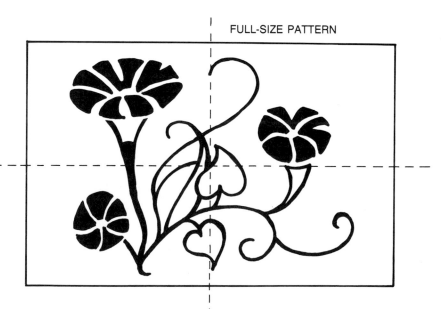

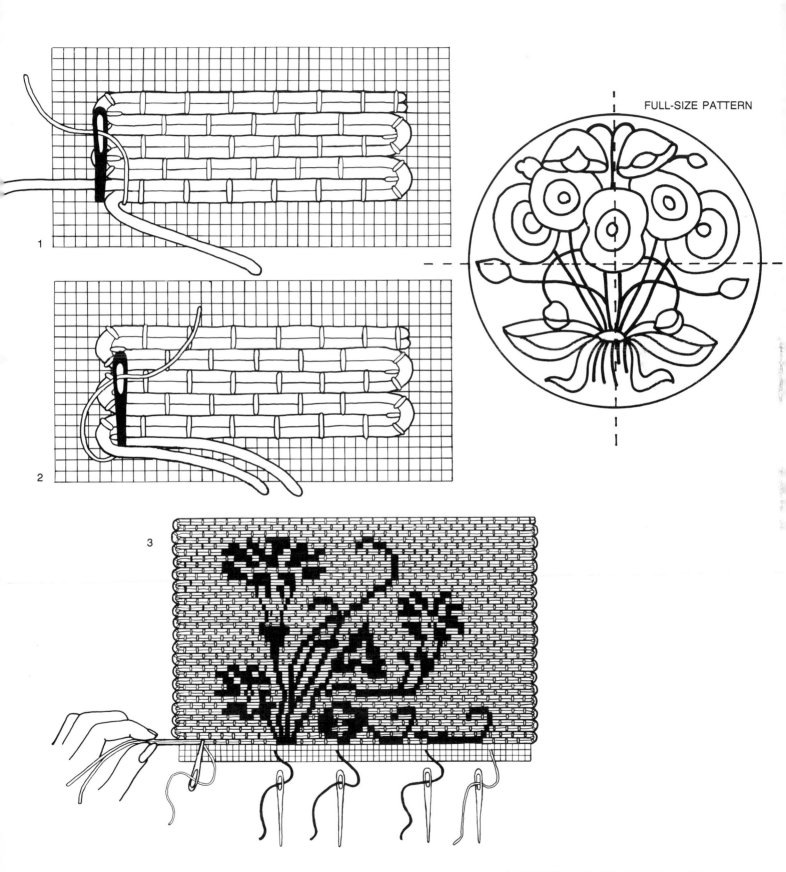

FULL-SIZE PATTERN

1

2

3

(Color photo, page 113.)

SHOPPING LIST
¼ yard 30-mesh gauze
2 yards 1½"-wide bias satin fabric
silk or cotton floss
Japanese gold thread
satin or silk lining fabric

LOTUS PETAL COLLAR

Inspired by a magnificent mandarin Chinese costume of the seventeenth century, this collar is made in the *Or Nué* technique described on the previous page. It can be edged with any color fabric and made with any number of petals.

Trace the full-size pattern for the petals onto gauze, leaving at least eight threads around each for turnbacks. Work in the *Or Nué* technique (page 127), using one thread of Japanese gold. Start couching across the broadest area to more easily establish the design, and fill in corner points afterwards. If you prefer the look of the lower collar in the photograph, you can work the background in Chinese openwork (page 145) and the flowers in long and short stitches, outlining them in couched gold thread. Trim completed needlework, leaving ¼" turnbacks.

Outline the two neckband patterns on satin. Work a border of Pekinese stitch at the top and bottom of the upper band and the bottom only of the lower band. Between the rows, work woven spiders' webs and clusters of three french knots. Trim the finished bands, leaving ¼" turnbacks.

Stitch the lower band, rights sides facing, to the top of the center petal. Bind around the edges of the petal and the band with a bias strip of satin, leaving the top unfinished. If you wish, work decorative stitching (backstitch, whipped chain, etc.) on the binding afterwards.

Bind the remaining two petals in the same way, leaving the top unfinished and at least 2" of extra binding at both outside edges. Stitch the upper band across the tops of petals, right sides facing, and finish the binding along the sides of the upper band.

Position the center petal behind the others as in the photograph and slip stitch it in place. Cut a piece of satin or contrasting silk lining to cover the entire back of the collar. Turn under raw edges and slip stitch the lining in place. Starting at the center of the upper band and working out to each side, finish along the top with a 30"-long bias strip. Use the bias strip that extends from the sides to tie the collar at the neck.

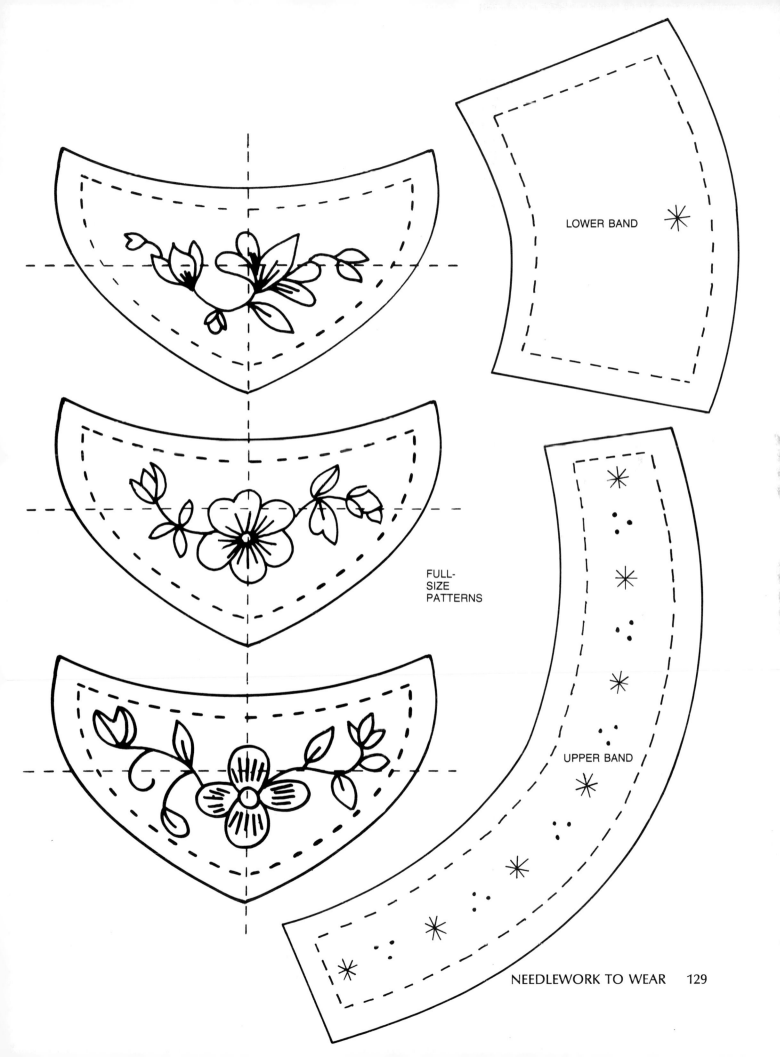

LOWER BAND

FULL-
SIZE
PATTERNS

UPPER BAND

NEEDLEWORK TO WEAR   129

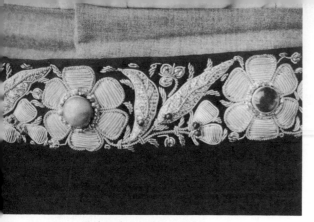

(Color photo, page 107.)

SHOPPING LIST
mock suede fabric
cornplasters
metallic thread
stones for needlework
  (with holes for stitching to fabric)
interfacing
lining fabric

JEWELLED BELT

Make your own adaptation of this Indian jewelled belt, splendid with cabuchon stones and raised gold threads. In order to raise the settings of the stones, you must pad with felt and the ideal shape for this turned out to be cornplasters! Since they adhere to the suede fabric and can be completely covered with lazy daisy stitches in metallic thread, no one will ever know the secret of your success!

Mount your fabric on stretcher strips. Trace the flower medallion and arrange it with leaves or cords, as you prefer. Put self-adhesive cornplasters in place for the flower centers. Cover the cornplasters with satin stitch. Work large lazy daisy stitches on top (Diagram 1). Fill the centers of the lazy daisy stitches with satin stitch (optional). Sew the stones in the centers. Work embroidered leaves or couch gold cord around the flowers (Diagram 2). Trim the finished emboidery, leaving ¼" turnbacks. Cut interfacing to exact size and fold turnbacks to reverse side over it. Hem the lining in place to finish the belt.

FULL-SIZE PATTERN (1 REPEAT)

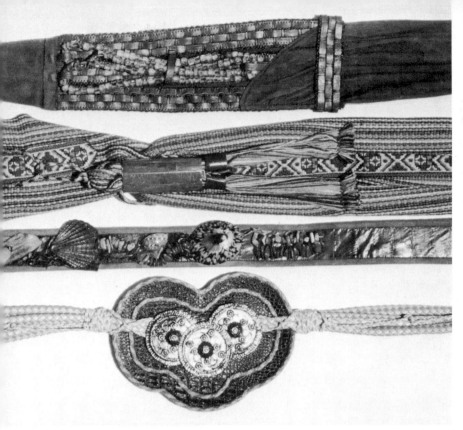

(Color photo, page 107.)

(Color photo, page 112.)

DESIGNER BELTS

Belts by South American designer Lisandro Sarasola show how you can use many of the techniques in this book and experiment with your own imaginative designs. Take advantage of natural materials such as shells, stones, leather, suede, jute, and even bones.

For instance, you could couch strips of leather or "Swade" in brick stitch on canvas like the top belt. Then mount the completed couched section into a gathered band of suede cloth and string found objects such as shells, bones, or beads on top.

The Middle Eastern influence has given us belts with wide and narrow bandings, wrapped to give a soft waistline. This is illustrated by the second belt of decorative webbings. You might take a narrow embroidered ribbon and apply it to a broader band of fabric to frame it. Ends can be fringed, knotted, and tied.

In the third belt, shells and stones have been applied to leather. Collect shells with natural holes and sew them down with waxed thread to a needlepoint belt. Glue stones with epoxy to buttons with flat tops and small shanks and they will be easy to stitch in place.

The bottom belt is made with brass medallions on leather. You could follow the instructions for the Ecuador Gold Medallion on page 32 to make your own version of this belt, mounting the medallion on groups of braids made from leather, jute, or rattail cord.

QUICK & EASY

Add that personal touch with something you can make quickly and easily. Here are all kinds of ideas from cross-stitch buttons to frilled crocheted collars and cuffs, from a braided ribbon barrette to a bullion knot bracelet. You can knit an unusual lapel pin or can convert a casual sweatshirt into an elegant evening top with scarcely a stitch at all! Don't forget these projects when you need to whip up a last minute gift or an added touch for a special outfit.

BULLION KNOT PIN OR BRACELET

(Size 6 steel crochet hook, white Knit-Cro-Sheen yarn, embroidery floss, cardboard, small piece of white fabric, cotton.)

The crochet oval base for the pin or bracelet is worked in rounds. Join with a slip stitch at the end of each round and chain 1; do not turn.

Round 1: Ch 7, sc in second ch from hook and next 4 ch; 3 sc in last ch; working along other side of ch, sc in next 5 ch; 3 sc in next ch; join with ss to first sc (16 sc). Rounds 2-5: Sc around, inc 2 sc over inc at each end of last round. (4 sc added on each round. Total at end of round 5 is 32 sc). Round 6: Sc around, inc 8 sc evenly spaced. (40 sc.) Round 7: * Sc, ch 3, ss in sc just worked; sc, rep from * around. Join with ss. (20 picots formed.) After you have crocheted the oval, you are ready to embroider the flowers on top. They are worked in bullion knots with a variety of colored embroidery floss of your choosing. Between the bullion knot roses (page 147), work some green bullion knot leaves and scatter a few colorful French knots here and there as well. Next, cut an oval piece of cardboard to measure approximately 2" × 1¾". Cover the cardboard with white fabric and sew to secure.

This oval can be used as a pin or, following these instructions for the band, as a bracelet. Each link measures approximately 1". Work with three strands of yarn held together. The band is made of links of chain stitch. Each link has a center post and two outside chains, form-

ing an oval. Ch 12; ss into first ch; ch 6, ss into 6th ch of ch 12. (First link of chain formed.) * Ch 11; ss into ss at end of last link. Ch 6; ss into 6th ch of ch 11. Rep from * for desired number of links. Bracelet shown has six links on either side of the oval.

If you are making a bracelet, tack the bands to the wrong side of the cardboard backing. Blind stitch the embroidered front to the back of the oval, leaving an opening. Stuff the oval firmly with cotton and finish sewing.

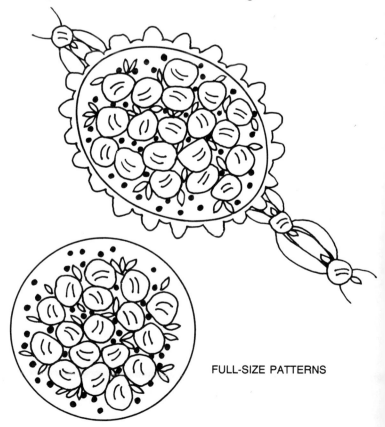

FULL-SIZE PATTERNS

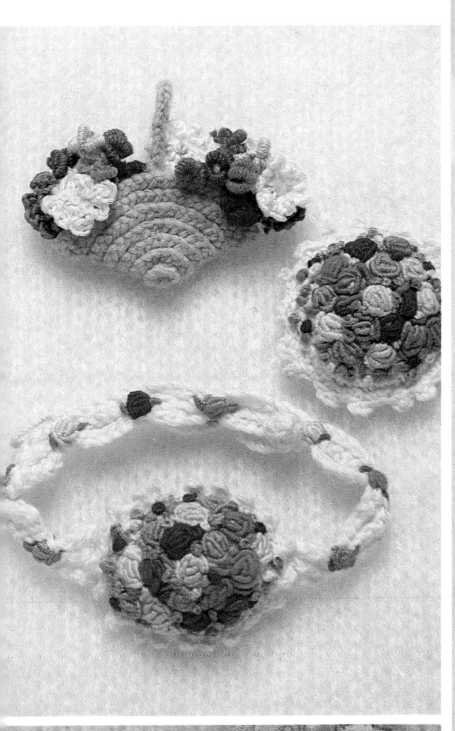

Above, left: BASKET OF FLOWERS *and* BULLION KNOT PIN
AND BRACELET. *Left:* CROCHET SWEATER EDGING.
Above: MINI SWEATER; DRAGONFLY, RUFFLE, *and* WRAPP
CORD COMBS.

Above: BRAIDED RIBBON BARRETTE, CROSS-STITCH BUTTONS, CROCHET BUTTONS, QUILTED VEST, RIBBON ROSES.

Opposite: CROCHET FLOWER NECKLACE, GOLD COLLAR, CROCHET RUFFLE COLLAR AND CUFFS, ROSE BUD SWEATER.

NEEDLEWORK TO WEAR   135

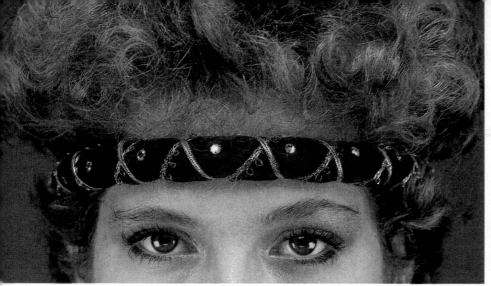

Make a wrapped and studded BROW BAND and beautifully decorated SWEAT SHIRTS with the help of a stud setter.

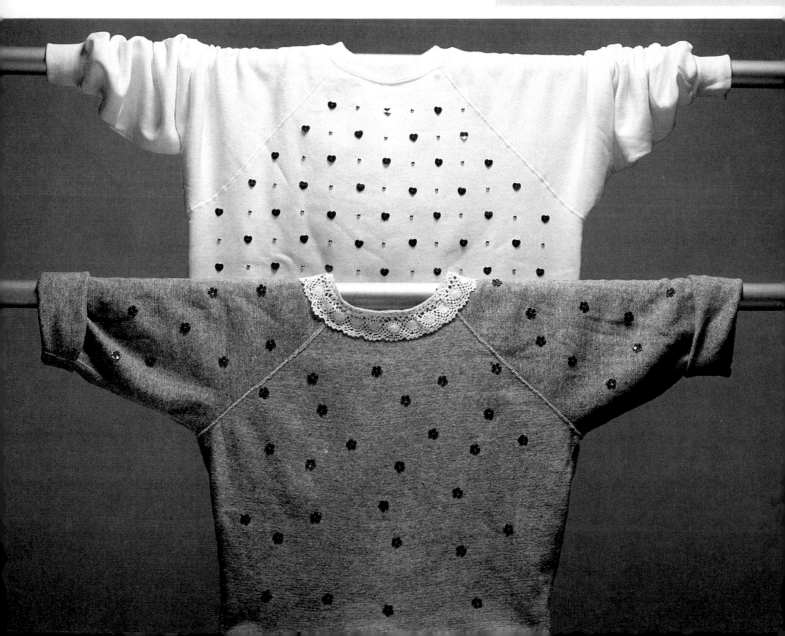

SWEAT SHIRTS

(Sweat shirt, rhinestone setter, studs, sequins.)

As universal as blue jeans, sweat shirts come in a wonderful variety of colors. Their soft fabric may be trimmed without raveling to make short sleeves and to add collars of lace or eyelet. The fabric is also a perfect background for any kind of decoration such as painting, embroidery, or even, as shown here, decorating with studs. Using a rhinestone setter which comes with an adaptor for setting studs, you do it all with scarcely a stitch! (See Suppliers.)

My daughter Jessica designed these sweat shirts, setting the studs and interspersing them with sequin hearts held with a single stitch. To space studs and sequins evenly, baste graph paper to the reverse side of the sweat shirt and mark the position of each stud. The studs are set from the back, so no marks will show on the front. Accuracy is important—no unpicking is possible!

BROW BANDS

(22" square of fabric, rhinestone setter, studs, gold cord.)

The velvet band is studded with sequins in the same way as the sweat shirts. Begin with a narrowly hemmed 22" square of fabric. (Bandanas can also be used.) Fold it in half diagonally, wrong sides together. Space studs as desired along the center 12" of the diagonal, about ½" in from the fold. Roll the fabric from corner toward fold to make a tube. Wrap the center 12" with gold cord.

CROCHET BUTTONS

Work these buttons in rounds; do not join.
Ch 2. Round 1: Work 6 sc into second ch from hook. Round 2: Work 2 sc in each sc (12 sc). Rounds 3 and 4: Work even on 12 sc.

Stuff button firmly. Round 5: Work 2 tog around (6 sc). Sew button shut. Sew button to top of right front and work a ch 8 loop at top of left front.

For larger buttons, or when working with fine threads, work more rows around.

BRAIDED RIBBON BARRETTE

(Double-bar barrette, one yard each of two colors of Offray ⅛-wide satin or grosgrain ribbon.)

Open the barrette. Lay the ribbons side by side and fold them in half to find their centers. Place those centerpoints in the folded hinge of the barrette. The four lengths of ribbon that now extend from the sides should be the same length (Diagram 1).

Take both ribbons from one side and slide them through gap between the two bars, pulling them through on the opposite side. Repeat with the second set of ribbons. Push this completed braid just over the folded hinge to the back of the barrette.

Take one ribbon from either side and thread it through the gap. Then take the same color from the other side, threading it the other way. Repeat this process with the two ribbons in the second color. (Diagram 2). Be sure to pull ribbons tight.

Keep braiding in this manner until the barrette is covered. At the end of the barrette, tie the remaining ribbons in a double knot. Leave the ends hanging.

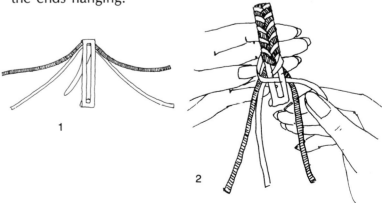

1

2

ROSE BUD SWEATER

(Any sweater, heavy yarn, interfacing.)

The store-bought turquoise sweater is decorated with bullion knot roses made from bold-scale wool. Instead of stitching the bullion knots directly on the sweater, stitch them first on interfacing (black for dark colors, white for light). When each rose is completed, trim away the excess interfacing close to the embroidery. Position the roses on the sweater and stitch them in place so none of the interfacing shows.

GOLD COLLAR

(Gold Camelot yarn, size 0 crochet hook.)

This soft crochet collar drapes beautifully on almost anything from a sweater to a dress.

Ch 112. Row 1: Hdc in third ch from hook and each rem ch (110 hdc). Ch 2, turn. Row 2: Hdc in each hdc of Row 1, ch 4, turn. Row 3: Dc in next 2 sts, ch 1, * dc in next 3 sts, ch 1, rep from * across row, ending with dc in last 2 sts. (Turning chain counts as first dc, 110 dc.) Ch 7, turn. Row 4: 2 tr in first ch 1 space, * ch 3, 2 tr in next ch 1 space, rep from * across, ending with ch 3. Tr in turning ch of Row 3, ch 1, turn.

Row 5: 3 sc in ch 3 space, * sc in next 2 tr, 3 sc in ch 3 space, sc in next 2 tr, ch 3, turn; skip sc at base of ch, then dc in next 6 sc, ch 3, turn; skip dc at base of ch, dc in next 2 dc; ch 4, sl st in first ch (ch 4 loop formed), dc in next 4 dc; sl st in side of dc just worked, 2 sl sts inside of dc below the one just worked. Then 3 sc in next ch 3 space of Row 4. Rep from * across. (18 motifs formed.) End with 3 sc in last space, ch 11, turn.

Row 6: Sc in first ch 4 loop, * ch 11, sc in next ch 4 loop, rep from * across, ending with sc in last sc of row below. (19 ch 11 loops formed.) Ch 1, turn. Row 7: Work 11 sc over each ch 11 loop of row 6, end off.

Work a crochet button from the instructions on page 137 and sew it to the top of the right front. Work a chain 8 loop at the top of the left front.

RIBBON ROSES

(Double-faced satin ribbons approximately 1" wide, dark on one side and light on the other, are ideal for this project.)

Roll one end of ribbon about six turns to make a tight tube. Bend base of tube up slightly and sew a few stitches to hold. This forms the center of the rose. (Diagram 1.)

To make petals, continue turning ribbon end toward you, folding ribbon down so its edge is lined up with tube (Diagram 2). Roll tube across ribbon end to form a cone; wind folded ribbon around tube. When tube lies parallel to remaining ribbon, take a few stitches to hold the petal you just made (Diagram 3). Keep folding ribbon over in the same direction to make alternately light and dark petals.

Continue making petals until rose is desired size, shaping the rose as you work and sewing each petal to base of rose. If you wind tightly, buds are formed. Looser petals make full-blown roses; narrow ribbon forms rosettes.

Finish by folding ribbon end over so the end is on the stitched base. Sew end to base; trim excess ribbon to about 1". Sew the rose in the desired position or slip a piece of fine wire through the stitches, winding around base of flower to secure and then forming the stem from remaining wire. If desired, add leaves available in notions or novelty stores (Diagram 4).

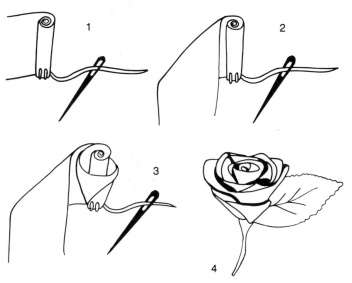

CROSS-STITCH BUTTONS

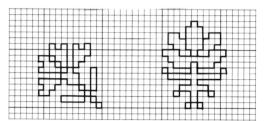

(16-count Aida cloth, cotton floss, self-covering button kit.)

These cross-stitch buttons are the finishing touch for a handmade sweater or blouse. Counting from the graphs, cross-stitch the pattern onto the fabric, choosing either the flowers or the alphabet. Following the instructions on the kit, mount the buttons, being careful to center each design.

Use the buttons to finish a sweater, stitch them to a macrame band to form a necklace, or add them as the finishing touch to a quilted or needlepoint belt buckle.

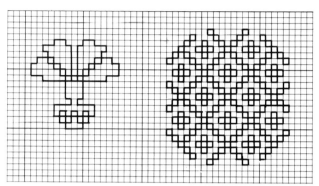

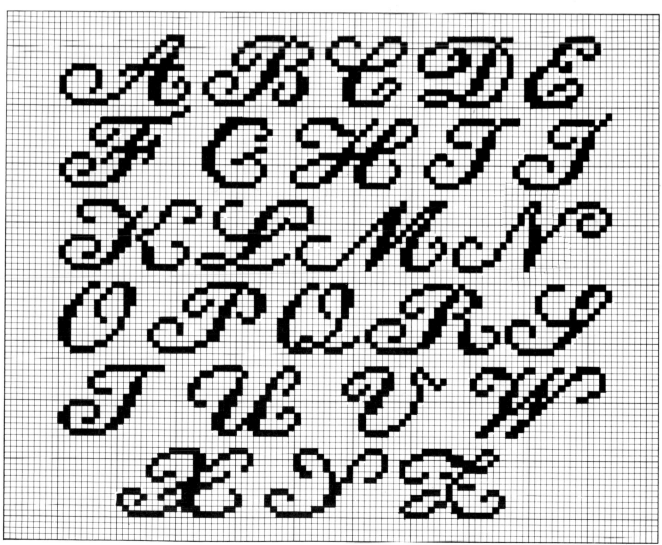

FLOWER NECKLACE

(One ball Knit-Cro-Sheen yarn, size 6 steel crochet hook.)

This necklace is made of four different sizes of crocheted flowers, the size being determined by the number of rounds completed. The smallest flower measures about 1" across.

Make four A flowers (rounds 1-3); two B flowers (rounds 1-7); and one D flower (rounds 1-9).

For each flower, ch 4 and join to form ring. Round 1: * ch 2, 2 dc in ring, ch 2, ss in ring. Rep from * four times. (4 petals made.) Round 2: Ss into back of first petal; * ch 2, ss into back of petal, rep from * five times, evenly spaced around. (5 loops.) Round 3: Ss, ch 2, 2 dc, ch 2, ss into each loop around. (5 petals.) Round 4: Ss into back of first petal of previous round. * Ch 3, ss into back of petal. Rep from * six times, evenly spaced around. (6 loops.) Round 5: Ss, ch 2, 3 dc, ch 2, ss into each loop around. (6 petals.)

Round 6: Ss into back of first petal of previous round. * ch 3, ss into back of petal. Rep from * eight times, spaced around. (8 loops.) Round 7: Ss, ch 2, 4 dc, ch 2, ss into each loop around. (8 petals.) Round 8: Ss into back of first petal of previous round. * Ch 3, ss into back of petal. Rep from * eleven times, evenly spaced around. (11 loops.) Round 9: Ss, ch 2, 5 dc, ch 2, ss into each loop around. (11 petals.)

Join flowers together by sewing two petals of one to two petals of the next in the following order: A, A, B, C, D, C, B, A, A. The center flower (D) should be joined closer to its top so it will hang lower than the others. Join the yarn to the free side of one end flower (A) and work the chain as follows: Ch 12; ss into joining; ss into 6th ch of ch-12. (First link formed.) * Ch 11; ss into ss at end of last link; ch 6; ss into 6th ch of ch-11. Rep from * four times. Ch 6; ss to first ch to form loop for button; work 11 sc over loop. Work the other side of the chain in the same manner, omitting button loop. Make a crochet button (page 137) and sew it to the end.

QUILTED VEST

(Prequilted fabric, silk or cotton floss.)

Using prequilted fabric or even mattress padding, follow the quilted outline with chain stitch, using either one or several colors of floss. Intertwine this lattice pattern with a climbing vine in stem stitch, with roses in bullion knots and leaves in lazy daisy stitch. A vest, jacket, or tabard top is quickly made by finishing the edges with a bias binding in the predominating color, using the same binding for ties as well. (Prequilted fabric is available in all colors.)

CROCHET RUFFLE COLLAR & CUFFS

(1 ball Annie Blatt, Sweet Anny yarn or Darling yarn, size 0 crochet hook.)

You could easily adapt this lovely ruffle pattern, shown here as collar and cuffs on a sweater, to make a shawl. A delightful tiered effect is acheived by attaching several overlapping rows.

To make the collar, ch 61. Row 1: Sc into second ch from hook and ch across (60 st). Row 2: Work (dc, ch 1, dc) into every other stitch of last row ("V" stitch). Row 3: Work (dc, ch 1) four times in each "V" of last row. Row 4: Work 3 dc into every other ch 1 space of last row.

For cuffs, ch 31 and rep as above. To knit the sweater, see instructions on page 64.

DRAGONFLY HAIR COMB

(Japanese gold thread, size 1 crochet hook, clear
   plastic comb, clear nylon thread.)

For the body, ch 8; sc in second ch from
hook and each rem ch (7 sc). Cut yarn, leaving
3" tail at beg of ch and end of sc row for
feelers. Tie knot at base of each feeler for eyes.

For the wings, ch 10; ss in first ch to form
loop for first wing; ch 13, ss in tenth ch from
the hook to form loop for other wing; ch 3,
turn. Row 1: Wk 5 dc in ch, then wk 2 dc at
end of loop, going into the loop instead of ch.
Ch 1, turn. Row 2: Wk sc in each dc and top
of turning ch (8 sc). Ss into center st on side of
butterfly body (being careful to have head in
right direction). Then work 3 sc into ch between wing loops (working *behind* butterfly
body); ss into center st on other side of body.
Do not turn.

Row 3: Ch 2; wk 5 dc into bottom of ch of
other wing, then 2 dc into end of loop, ch 1,
turn. Row 4: Sc in each dc and, turning ch (8
sc), slip ss into sc row behind butterfly body.

Attach the butterfly to the comb with clear
nylon thread.

COMB WITH RUFFLE

(Silver Camelot yarn, size 1 crochet hook, clear
   plastic comb, clear nylon thread.)

Ch 51. Row 1: Sc in second ch from hook
and each rem ch. Rows 2 and 3: Ch 1, turn,
sc in each sc. Row 4: Ch 4, turn; work dc in
first sc (ch 4 plus dc counts as first V st); work
dc, ch 1, dc in each sc across (50 V st). Sew
to comb with nylon thread, gathering as you
sew.

WRAPPED CORD COMB

(Heavy cord or clothes line, flat silver and gold
   cord, all-purpose glue, clear plastic comb,
   clear nylon thread.)

Cut heavy cord the exact length of the
comb. Wrap and glue around it alternating silver and gold cords. Allow to dry. With clear
nylon thread, oversew cords to top of comb.

BASKET OF FLOWERS

(Yarn, sewing thread, metal-core candlewicking,
   perle cotton, cotton floss.)

These flower baskets can be made in every
color and filled with flowers as varied as your
imagination allows. Begin by making a braid
from yarn. Sew it in a circle as you would a
braided rug (Diagram 1). Fold the circle in half
and sew a braid handle on top (Diagram 2).

Wrap the candlewicking with green floss,
knot the top (Diagram 3), and sew yarn petals
through it to form a flower head (Diagram 4).
Make other flowers by buttonholing with floss
or perle cotton in a ring around the center knot
or by making bullion knots (Diagram 5). Stitch
the stems in place, adding lazy daisy leaves.

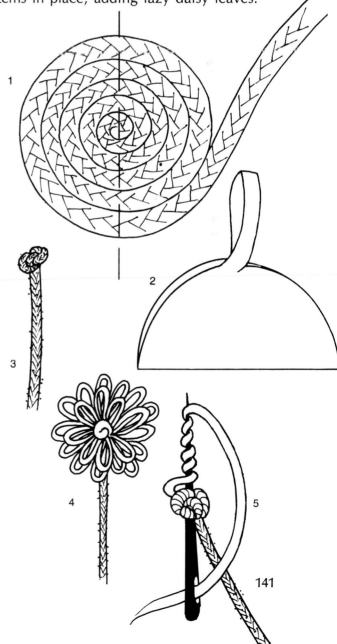

141

MINI SWEATER

(Size 5 knitting needles, worsted weight yarn.)

Worn as a pin, this adorable little sweater could be knitted in almost any size and in any yarn. Touches of embroidery could be added, or even the wearer's initials.

Cast on 12 sts. Rows 1-4: K 12. Rows 5-12: K one row, p the next, etc., ending with a p row. Row 13: Cast on 6 at beg of row and k 18. Row 14: Cast on 6 sts, then k 2, p 20, k 2. Row 15: k 24. Row 16: K 2, p 20, k 2. Row 17: K 24. Row 18: K 2, p 6, bind off 8 k sts, p 6, k 2. Row 19: K 8, cast on 8, k 8. Row 20: K 2, p 6, k 8, p 6, k 2. Row 21: k 24. Row 22: K 2, p 20, k 2. Row 23: K 24. Row 24: K 2, p 20, k 2.

Row 25: Bind off 6 sts, k 16. Row 26: Bind off 6 sts, k 12. Rows 27-33: K one row, p the next, etc., ending with a k row. Rows 34-37: K 12. Bind off.

Sew side seams. Wind a small ball of yarn, leaving a 12" length loose. With a tapestry needle, run the loose end in and out of the ball a few times until it holds. Allowing the ball to dangle, secure the yarn at the shoulders to form a loop for a hanger. Work toothpicks through the neck edge for needles.

CROCHET SWEATER EDGING

(Rayon ribbon or silky seam binding, size B or C crochet hook.)

Used on a Chanel-type knitted jacket or a sweater, this clever edging by Ruth Rohn makes a casual sweater elegant for evening. Begin by working into the knitted edge of the sweater to make a foundation row of chain stitch all around. Turn the work to begin working into this first foundation row. Work one chain; then insert the hook into the third chain from the hook. Work one double crochet. Insert the hook, going back into the previous chain (immediately before the double crochet stitch) and work one single crochet into this chain. Then work a second single crochet into the same stitch. Now work one chain and repeat from the beginning, working one double crochet into the third chain from the hook.

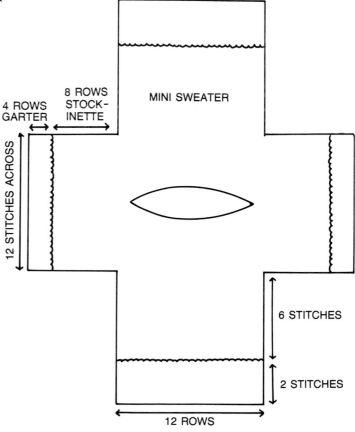

4 ROWS GARTER

8 ROWS STOCK-INETTE

MINI SWEATER

12 STITCHES ACROSS

6 STITCHES

2 STITCHES

12 ROWS

ENLARGING & REDUCING

Most patterns in this book have been given in actual size. If a design does need enlarging or reducing, the best method is to have a photostat made. Photostat services are available in most towns (check your yellow pages under photocopying or blueprint services). Give one finished measurement, height or width, and the drawing will be enlarged proportionately.

Another method that can easily be done at home, at no expense, is enlarging by the squaring method. Generally, the simpler the design, the fewer the squares that will be needed. First divide your design into squares as shown. Then take a piece of paper the size the enlargement is to be and fold it into the same number of squares. (This is easier than measuring.) Draw the design square by square to fit within them.

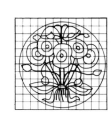

USING A FRAME

Most needlework is worked better and more easily if the background material is stretched really tight in order to keep the stitches even. To mount your work, remove the outer hoop of the frame. Adjust the screw so the outer hoop fits snugly over the inner ring and material. Place material over the inner ring, centering area to be worked. Pull fabric taut, pressing the outer hoop down. If it is tight enough, the material will not slip back. Working with both hands, one always below the frame and the other above, pass the needle back and forth vertically through the material. To remove the hoop, do not unscrew; press thumbs down on work while lifting off outer hoop with fingers.

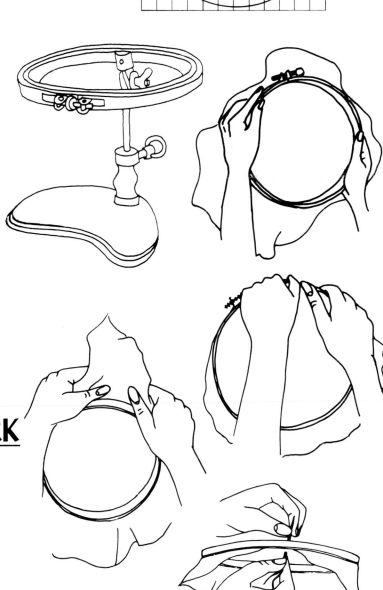

BLOCKING FINISHED WORK

The best method for blocking finished needlework is by stretching it over artists' stretcher strips. This allows both sides of the work to remain exposed for cleaning and quick drying. Purchase strips large enough to fit around the outside of the needlework. Mark center of each strip with a pencil and assemble them so that each corner is a right angle. Mark the center of each side of the needlework and place the needlework on top of the stretcher frame, right side up. Matching centers, staple the four sides, stretching work tightly as you do so. Then staple the corners. Continue stretching and stapling around opposite sides until staples are ¼" apart and work is stretched square and tight. Run cold water over needlework and wash gently if it is soiled. Prop the frame up and let the needlework dry.

TRANSFERRING

The method you choose for transferring your design is determined by the type of material you will be working on. Choose the most suitable one for your purpose.

Always prepare fabric for design transfer as follows: Cut the fabric on the straight of the grain, allowing ample extra fabric for mounting and backing. Fold the material in half vertically right down the center and repeat this horizontally. Crease the folds firmly or baste lines on fabric. Repeat this on your paper pattern; then, while you lay one on top of the other, align the lines to keep design centered.

BACK LIGHTING
(For medium-weight linen or cotton, velvet, delicate fabrics and blends.)

Stretch fabric onto artist's stretcher strips and staple or tack. Tape a boldly traced design to the reverse side, close to the fabric. Place a lamp behind the frame so a clear silhouette of the design shines through. Trace with a fine-tipped permanent marker. (You can also tape the design and then the fabric to an artist's lightbox and trace.)

CARBON PAPER
(For medium-weight linen or cotton.)

Use *only* dressmaker's carbon—blue for light materials, white or yellow for dark. Working on a smooth hard surface, slide a sheet of carbon face down between the paper and fabric. Anchor the paper with weights and, with smooth flowing lines, trace the outline very heavily with a pencil.

TRACE ERASE™ PEN
(For all fabrics)

This marking pen transfers with a blue line which can be erased by touching with cold water. It is ideal for freehand drawing because unwanted lines will completely disappear after the needlework is complete. Never apply heat before removing blue lines or they will become permanent.

NET METHOD
(For medium-weight linen or cotton, boldweave textured fabrics, wool, suede cloth.)

Trace the design on paper. Tape a piece of net over the drawing. Trace the design onto the net with broad-tipped permanent marker. Tape the net onto material. Retrace the design with the marker, which will penetrate through the net and mark the material. Test first to determine the correct line width.

TRACING
(For canvas and evenweave fabrics, organdy.)

Tape transparent fabrics directly over the design on a smooth surface. Lightly trace the design with a hard pencil. Similarly, tape needlepoint canvas over a boldly drawn design. Use fine *permanent* marker to trace the design onto canvas.

GRAPHS
(For canvas and evenweave fabrics.)

Some designs are counted directly from a graph onto canvas or evenweave fabric. Always work from the center out, counting the threads of the fabric—not the holes. One graph square represents one stitch.

WASTE CANVAS
(For most fabrics except canvas, evenweave fabrics, and organdy.)

Baste waste canvas over the design area of the fabric and mount both in an embroidery frame. Stitch through both thicknesses as described under *Graphs*. When the design is finished, unravel the canvas threads at edges and draw them right out, one by one. If fabric is washable, soaking in cold water loosens threads, allowing them to slip out more easily.

FUSIBLE WEB
(For most fabrics except canvas, evenweave fabrics, and delicate fabrics and blends.)

Trace the design onto web with a permanent marker and mount the web with the fabric in an embroidery frame. Baste the web in position. Work the design over both layers. When finished, tear web away. Remove remaining bits by rubbing with flat end of scissors.

TAILOR'S CHALK
(For medium-weight linen or cotton, boldweave textured fabrics, wool, and suede cloth.)

Draw the design freehand, directly on fabric. Mistakes can be rubbed off.

BASTING
(For canvas, woven fabrics, heavy fabrics, piles and knits.)

Trace the design onto a transparent fabric such as organdy, using a hard pencil. Pin the transparent fabric with the tracing to the *wrong* side of fabric. Baste around all outlines with small running stitches and contrasting thread, which will transfer design to the right side. Work over the stitches or draw them out later.

STITCHES

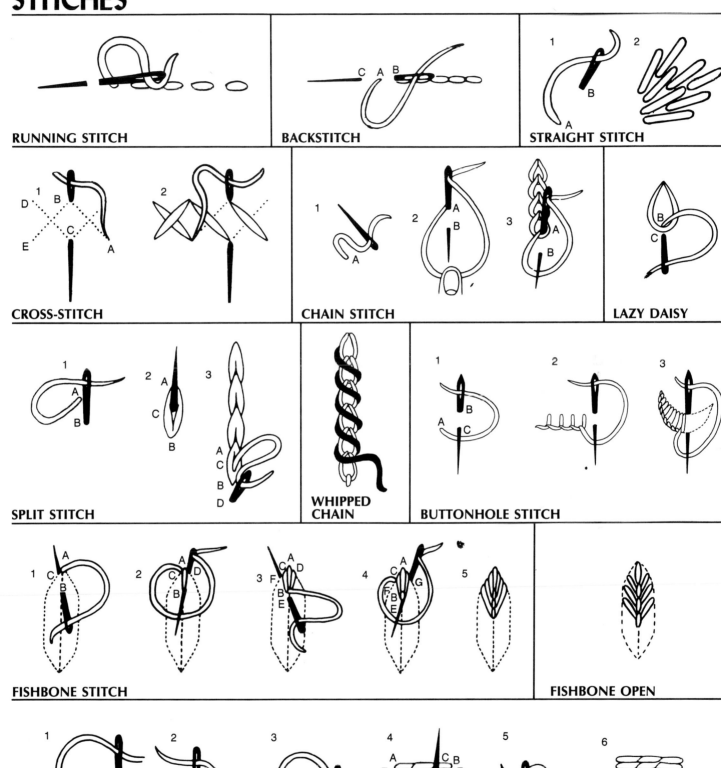

RUNNING STITCH

BACKSTITCH

STRAIGHT STITCH

CROSS-STITCH

CHAIN STITCH

LAZY DAISY

SPLIT STITCH

WHIPPED CHAIN

BUTTONHOLE STITCH

FISHBONE STITCH

FISHBONE OPEN

ROUMANIAN STITCH

HERRINGBONE STITCH

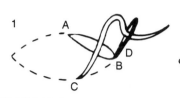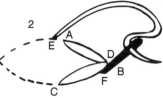

CLOSE HERRINGBONE

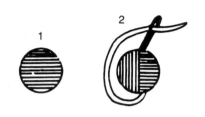

SATIN STITCH	SATIN WITH SPLIT STITCH	PADDED SATIN STITCH

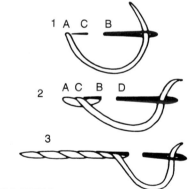

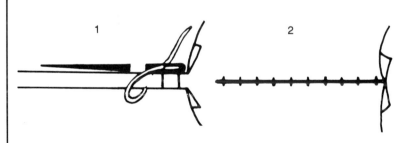

BLIND STITCH

STEM STITCH

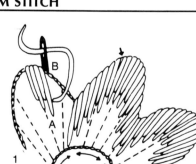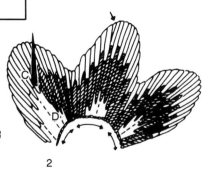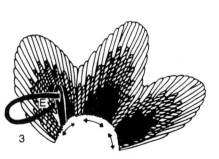

LONG AND SHORT STITCH

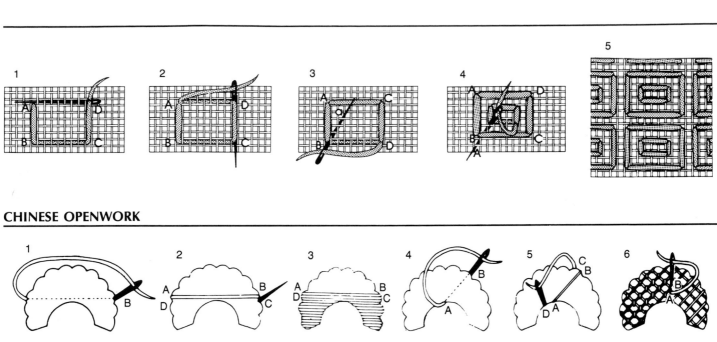

CHINESE OPENWORK

LAIDWORK

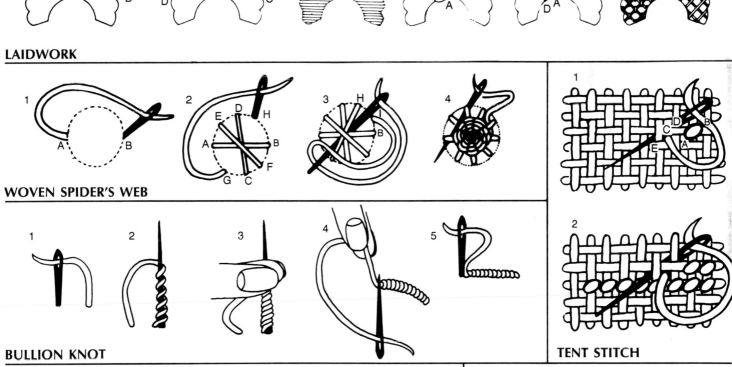

WOVEN SPIDER'S WEB

BULLION KNOT

TENT STITCH

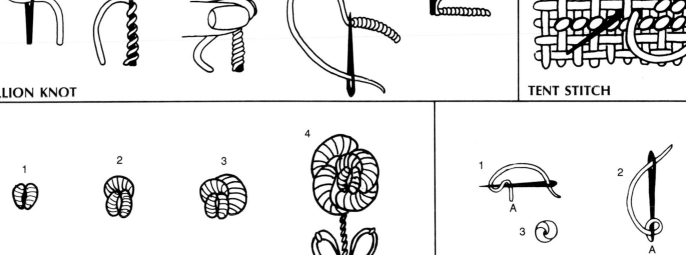

BULLION KNOT ROSES

FRENCH KNOT

SMOCKING STITCHES

Needle should always be horizontal.

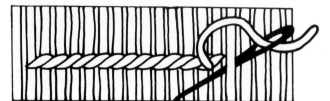

STEM   Work left to right. Hold thread above needle.

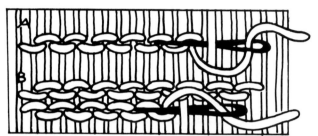

CABLE   Work left to right. Hold thread alternately above and below needle.

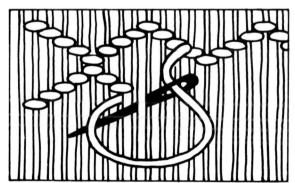

CHEVRON   Work left to right. Work five stitches with thread below needle, five stitches with the thread above. (The fifth stitch becomes the first in the next group of five.)

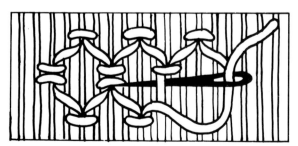

DIAMOND LATTICE   Work left to right. Take one reed at a time. Reverse direction on the second row to make a diamond pattern.

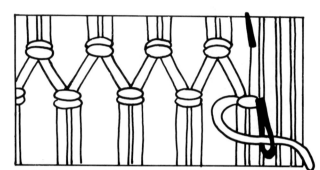

FEATHER   Work right to left. Take two reeds, holding thread under needle. Repeat, taking three down, three up to make a zigzag line.

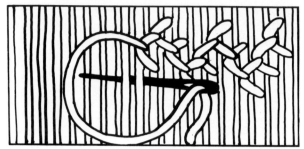

SPOT HONEYCOMB   Work left to right. Take two reeds together; slide needle through each reed to the next stitch.

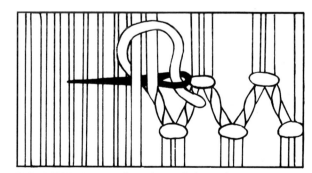

VAN DYKE   Work right to left. Take two reeds together, then one reed, then two together, across the row.

PATTERN FOR PAINTED SILK JACKET

Enlarge the pattern below with bold lines and trace it onto tracing paper. Repeat to make several blocks of flowers, which you can cut out and arrange on your jacket as you prefer. A suggested arrangement for the back, front, and sleeve is shown below. To paint and finish the jacket, follow the instructions on page 72.

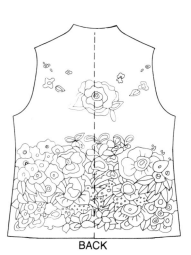

BACK

1 SQUARE = 2"

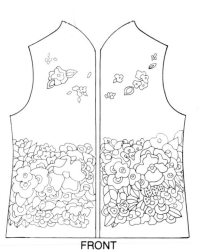

FRONT

SLEEVE

MOUNTING A HANDBAG

Complete the stitching for the front flap and, if necessary, couch the border and spine. Your worked design, including borders, is your guide for the bag's dimensions. Allow extra fabric for turnbacks.

If you are using a single-faced fabric, fuse two pieces together, wrong sides facing, with fusible web. Use this fused fabric to cut 2¼"-wide gussets for the bottom and both sides of the bag. Gusset length should be 1" longer than the applicable dimension from the needlework.

Allowing extra fabric for turnbacks, cut suede fabric for the back and the inside front. Stitching close to the edge of the needlework or border, machine stitch the back rectangle to the front flap, right sides facing. Lay this seamed piece face down on the table and finger press the seam towards the back.

Using a graph paper pattern, cut cardboard or illustration board the exact size of the seamed back piece. To help the board bend at the spine,

score the spine area several times with the points of scissors. Cut board the same way for the inside front.

With white glue, adhere the seamed back piece and the inside front to their boards. Fold the back piece into the envelope position and allow the glue to dry. Then, fold over glued turnbacks, mitering corners.

For the lining, substitute fusible interfacing for board and follow the procedure for the outside of the bag. Glue the lining pieces in place and allow the outside of the bag to dry in the envelope position as before. Machine stitch close to the top edge of the inside front piece to reinforce.

Establish and mark with pins the center points of the base and sides of the bag, front and back, as well as the center points of the gussets. Join the bag, matching pins, with ⅛" machine stitched seams. From the outside, neatly back stitch short gusset seams by hand. Trim the excess if necessary.

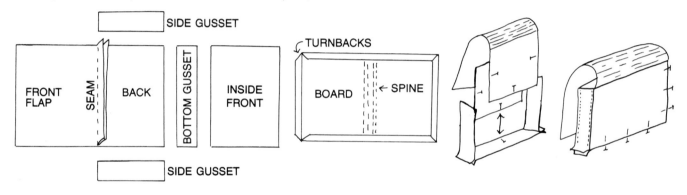

MAKING THE JEWEL CABINET

To make the Flowering Garden Jewel Cabinet (page 45), fold the finished, padded embroidery over pieces of cardboard. Following the procedure in Diagram 1, trim and miter corners of the fabric.

Placing the cardboard behind the fabric (Diagram 2), pin and hem a piece of lining fabric on the reverse side of each cardboard-lined pattern piece (Diagram 3).

With strong quilting or nylon sewing thread, sew the sections together (Diagram 4). (Diagram 5 shows the basic construction of the box.) Add a catch to close the doors of the cabinet and, if desired, stitch the small butterfly over it.

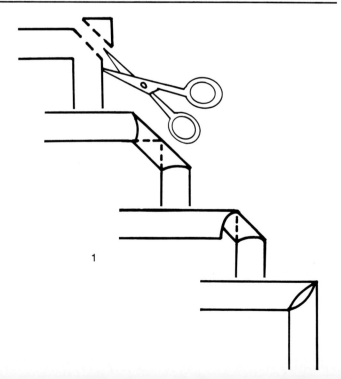

1

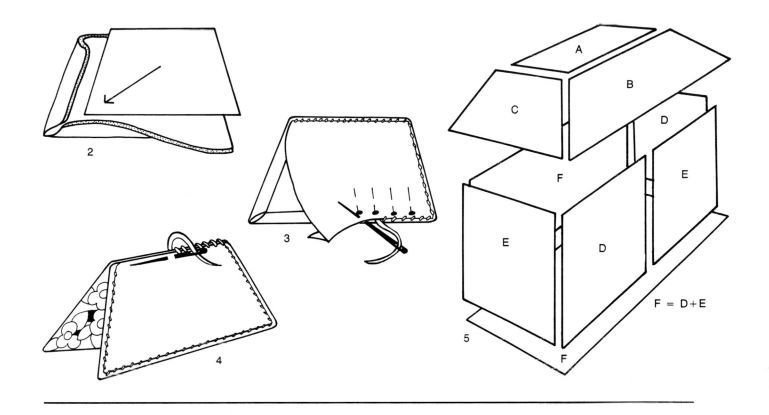

MAKING A TRAVELLING JEWEL CASE

Trim the finished needlework, leaving ¼" for turnbacks all around. Clip and notch the turnbacks.

Line the finished needlework with felt and sew piping around it (Diagram 1). Add a hinge of quilted fabric or grosgrain ribbon (Diagram 2). Sew a zipper around the top except the area where the hinge has been sewn (Diagram 3).

Cut a cardboard circle and place it on the wrong side of the top (Diagram 4). Then, slip stitch a circle of lining fabric over it to hold the cardboard in place and finish the inside of the top.

Sew piping around the top edge of the side and sew the hinge and the bottom of the zipper to the side. Line the bottom with felt and then sew piping around the edge. Sew the bottom to the sides. Line the bottom and the sides.

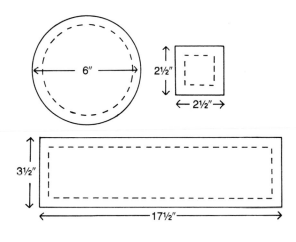

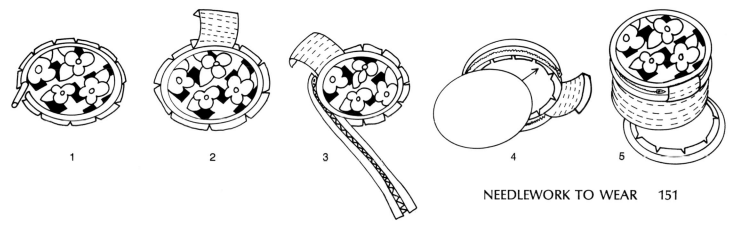

INDEX

SUPPLIERS

FABRICS

AIDA CLOTH, FIDDLERS CLOTH
*Sabra Supply Co.
P.O. Box 35575
Houston, Texas 77035

CHINA SILK FABRIC FOR PAINTING AND QUILTING
Paron Fabrics, Inc.
140 W. 57th Street
New York, New York 10019

FINE SILK GAUZE, NYLON GAUZE
Erica Wilson Needleworks
717 Madison Avenue
New York, New York 10021

*Kreinik
1351 Market Street
Parkersburg, West Virginia 26101

GOLD KID FABRIC, LACE (READY-MADE COLLARS)
M & J Trimming Co.
1008 6th Avenue
New York, New York 10018

SUEDE CLOTH (SINGLE-FACED "VERTI SUEDE")
*Solomon Bainnson Co.
129 W. 27th Street
New York, New York 10001

PAINTS AND PENS

PROCION DYES
Pylam Products Co., Inc.
1001 Stewart Avenue
Garden City, New York 11530

TRACE ERACE™ PEN
Erica Wilson Needleworks
717 Madison Avenue
New York, New York 10021

VERSATEX ACRYLIC PAINTS
Sam Flax
55 E. 55th Street
New York, New York 10022

*Siphon Art
Ignacio, California 94947

FAB-TEX ACRYLIC PAINTS
Stencil-Ease
P.O. Box 311
Jaffrey, New Hampshire 03452

RIBBONS

DOUBLE-FACED SATIN RIBBONS
*C. M. Offray & Son, Inc.
261 Madison Avenue
New York, New York 10016

SMOCKING SUPPLIES

*Little Miss Muffet
316 Nancy Lynn Lane
P.O. Box 10912
Knoxville, Tennessee 37919

THREADS

APPLETON WOOL (FINE ENGLISH CREWEL WOOL);
  GOLD THREADS SUCH AS JAPANESE GOLD,
  LUREX, MALTESE SEWING SILK (HORSETAIL)
Erica Wilson Needleworks
717 Madison Avenue
New York, New York 10021

AU VERA SOIE, PING LING SILK
*Kreinik
1351 Market Street
Parkersburg, West Virginia 26101

COTTON FLOSS, FIL D'OR, FIL D'ARGENT
*DMC
107 Trumbull Street
Elizabeth, New Jersey 07206

GOLD CORD, LAMEFLEX, LUREX, STARDUST LAMÉ
*La Lame, Inc.
1170 Broadway
New York, New York 10001

KANAGAWA JAPANESE GOLD THREAD
*YL Corporation
742 Genevieve, Suite L
Solana Beach, California 92075

METAL-CORE CANDLEWICKING
*Rauch Industries, Inc.
P.O. Box 609
Highway 321, South
Gastonia, North Carolina 28052

CRAVENELLA KNITTING YARN
*Melrose Yarn Co., Inc.
1305 Utica Avenue
Brooklyn, New York 11203

DARLING KNITTING YARN
*Unger
230 Fifth Avenue
New York, New York 10010

MISCELLANEOUS

BEADS AND STONES (JASPER, LAPIS, GARNET,
  PEARLS, RINESTONES), RHINESTONE SETTER
M & J Trimming Co.
1008 6th Avenue
New York, New York 10018

*Wholesalers who will supply addresses of retail
sources in your area.

CLOTHING PATTERNS
Vogue/Butterick
161 Avenue of the Americas
New York, New York 10013

NOTIONS AND FABRICS
Clothworld
Hancock Fabrics
House of Fabrics
Joanne Fabrics
So-Fro Fabrics

KNITTING WOOLS AND NEEDLEWORK SUPPLIES
Erica Wilson Needleworks
717 Madison Avenue
New York, New York 10017

Margot Gallery
26 W. 54th Street
New York, New York 10019

The Status Thimble
311 Primrose Road
Burlingame, California 94010

The Ugly Duckling
700 Welch Road
Palo Alto, California 94304

ACKNOWLEDGEMENTS

I wish to thank the following people who so graciously lent me their works of art for photography: Ruth Katz for the bracelets on page 8 and the bags on page 85; Viola Andrycich for the pansies on page 12 and the collar on page 111; Tanya Josefowitz for the dress on page 51; Ruth Rhone for the sweater border on page 133; Jessica Cushman for the sweatshirts on page 136; and Mira Green for the flowering branch necklace on page 14.

The blouses on pages 56-58 are used with kind permission of Bena Racine of Patchmakers, Inc. and are available as kits under the name of "Almost Ready to Wear" from Patchmakers, 920 Broadway, New York, New York 10010.

I greatly appreciate the patience of my daughter, Vanessa Kagan, and the following friends, all of whom posed as models: Lucy Bucknell, Sarah Butterwick, Beverly Cole, Charlotte Kappler, Elise Mischel, and Jane Salisbury.

Special thanks to all those who worked on preparing the book: Viola Andrycich, Elizabeth Kried, Madeline Strauss, Sonja Dagress, Francisca Alvarez, Luisa Cabrera, Donna Rothchild, and Beth King.

Editor: Maura C. Kennedy
Design: Viola Andrycich, Steve Logan, David Morrison
Photography: Seth Joel, cover photograph and all other photography with the following exceptions: Vladimir Kagan, page 7 upper right, page 54 upper left, page 61 upper right; Ted Kappler, page 14, page 61 lower right, page 81 lower right, page 112, page 134 center left; Peter Levy for *Good Housekeeping Magazine*, pages 56-58. Photo on page 60 is courtesy of *Family Circle Magazine*.
Production Manager: Jerry Higdon